'tis a very proud thing to be irish
BORROWED
FROM
the
O'DRISCOLL
LIBRARY
COBH
SKIBBEREEN
céad
míle
fáilte

P9-DVO-988

Bernard Shaw: Man and Writer

AUDREY WILLIAMSON

BERNARD SHAW: MAN AND WRITER

The Crowell-Collier Press, New York
Collier-Macmillan, Ltd., London

First Crowell-Collier Press Edition 1963
Library of Congress Catalog Card Number: 63-11106

Published simultaneously by Collier-Macmillan Limited, London

Hecho en los E.E.U.U.
Printed in the United States of America

Acknowledgments

FROM THE VAST amount of literature on Shaw, the biographer must make a necessary selection. I am myself most indebted to St. John Ervine's *Bernard Shaw: His Life, Work and Friends* (Constable, 1956) and *Theatrical Companion to the Plays of Shaw* by Raymond Mander and Joe Mitchenson (Rockliff, 1954), both monumental providers of facts; and also to *The Correspondence of Ellen Terry and Bernard Shaw* (Reinhardt and Evans, 1949), *Bernard Shaw and Mrs. Patrick Campbell: Their Correspondence,* edited by Alan Dent (Gollancz, 1952); The *Shaw-Barker Letters,* edited by C. B. Purdom (Phoenix House, 1956); and *Shaw and Molly Tompkins,* edited by Peter Tompkins (Blond, 1961).

The most valuable material, biographical and critical, is still, of course, Shaw's own published writings, scattered over many volumes, and named where possible, with other sources, in the text.

My personal gratitude is also due to Mr. Cyril Cusack, Dame Sybil Thorndike, Dame Flora Robson and the late Mr. Walter Hudd, who provided further material in the way of books, photographs or reminiscences.

Acknowledgment must also be made to the following for permission to quote from copyright material: the Public Trustee and Society of Authors in respect of Shaw's published plays and prefaces, *Sixteen Self Sketches, Pen Portraits and Reviews, Music in London* (3 vols.), *London Music;* Victor Gollancz, Ltd. (London) and Alfred A. Knopf, Inc. (New York), *Bernard Shaw and Mrs. Patrick Campbell: Their Correspondence* (edited by Alan Dent);

The Bodley Head, Ltd. (London), *The Ellen Terry-Bernard Shaw Correspondence;* Phoenix House, Ltd. (London), *The Shaw-Barker Letters* (edited by C. B. Purdom); Anthony Blond, Ltd. (London), *Shaw and Molly Tompkins* (edited by Peter Tompkins); and the British Drama League and Ivor Brown, editor of the Magazine *Drama, Shaw as Producer* by Sir Lewis Casson.

A.W.

Contents

Bernard Shaw: Man and Writer

Chapter 1

The Irish Inheritance

"I NEVER FELT inclined to write, any more than to breathe. It never occurred to me that my literary sense was exceptional: I gave everyone credit for it; for there is nothing miraculous in a natural faculty to the man who has it."

Shaw wrote this in 1901, when his pen had become a memorable and sharply-fashioned instrument, fluidly emitting a prose style of which the above extract is basically characteristic: simple, supple and rhythmic, with its use of heightened pause and punctuation. But in essence Shaw was right and propagating a truth of all great writing and composition; the faculties of literary and musical expression are inborn, and indeed must be in those cases of natural fecundity where the sheer body and scope of the artist's work seem to exceed the bounds of ordinary industry and mental activity. So with Shakespeare; so with Dickens; so with Mozart, Wagner and Shaw. And it is not by accident that one links the name of Shaw with two musicians whose works were throughout his life a profound stimulus to his imagination.

The fact is Shaw wrote his prose like a composer, and in particular an operatic composer, with the rhythms, cadences and sounds of the human voice in mind, and a use of colon and semicolon which he admitted was deliberately aimed to supplement and vary the comma and full point according to the natural breathing pauses in human speech. It is as a result of this that actors have always found the dialogue of his plays easy to learn and to speak, and audiences and readers have been able to grasp without difficulty certain intellectual or sociological arguments which are far deeper and more complex than those they normally absorb.

A born writer, like a born composer, must nevertheless acquire tools and learn to handle them; and he must also develop ideas, the basic materials on which the tools work. In this his early background and contacts will inevitably have some latent influence; they are the roots from which, watered by life and practice, will emerge the creative tree. In this sense it is interesting to compare the backgrounds of Shaw and Wagner, both artists whose immense body of creative work was equaled in extent by their output of pamphlets, essays and criticism, not only on the subject of their art but on politics, philosophy, religion and other arts.

This profusion of talents and interests may have been partly inherited or inborn, but it sprang too from an early upbringing which in the case of Shaw and Wagner shows a curious reversal. It was Shaw, not Wagner, who was brought up in an atmosphere of music; Wagner, the stepson of an actor and younger brother of several stage players, spent all his early formative years steeped in drama, and his ambition right up to adolescence was to write tragedies like those of Shakespeare and the Greek dramatists. In a sense he achieved his ambition, for his early dramatic interests, through his librettos, took a vital part in his later work as a musician, just as Shaw himself, as a dramatist, continually reverted to the *Don Giovanni* myth (and especially the great "statue" scene of "my idol Mozart", as he called him) which had made such an impression on him in his musical youth.[1]

It was his mother, not his father, who provided Shaw with the musical passion and contacts that were to stimulate so much of his work as a writer, generating 'Corno

[1] For a fuller study of Wagner's influence on Shaw, see "Wagner and Shaw: A Dramatic Comparison," by Audrey Williamson in *Music Review,* Ed. Geoffrey Sharp, Pub. Heffer, Cambridge, August, 1958.

di Bassetto' and some of the most knowledgeable and witty volumes of music criticism in our language, in addition to a book, *The Perfect Wagnerite,* which stands alongside *The Quintessence of Ibsenism* as a surviving illumination of the work of a master.

The mother, Lucinda Elizabeth Gurly (a name which St. John Ervine in his biography of Shaw suggests may have derived from the Cumberland family of Gourlay), was the daughter of an Irish country gentleman, Walter Bagnal Gurly, of improvident habits and small estate. This Walter Gurly had married the daughter of another Irish country gentleman named Whitcroft, infinitely more solid in substance and property but tainted by extreme doubt as to his legitimacy and, almost worse, by some unmentionable if lucrative professional activities as a pawnbroker in Dublin. He had, however, married into what Shaw describes as "a genuine county family," and Shaw's mother was brought up "with ruthless strictness to be a paragon of all lady-like virtues and accomplishments by her grand aunt." The aunt was remembered by Shaw as a humpbacked old lady with a pretty face, to whom he was taken on a visit as a child in the apparent hope—not realized—that his infant charms would induce her to leave him some of her valuable property.

"When my mother grew up," wrote Shaw in *Sixteen Self Sketches,* published in 1949 when he was ninety-three years old, "she knew thoroughbass as taught by her music-master Johann Bernhard Logier (famous in Dublin as the inventor of the chiroplast, a mechanical finger exerciser which set his pupils all wrong); she could repeat two of La Fontaine's fables in French with perfect pronunciation; she could carry herself with complete dignity; and she could have worked as a ragpicker without losing her entire conviction that she was a lady, of a species apart from servants and common persons. But she could not house-keep on a small income; she had no notion of the value of money; she detested her grand aunt and regarded all that had been taught her as religion and discipline as tyranny and slavery. Consequently, as she was naturally very humane, she abandoned her own children to the most complete anarchy."

It happened to be rather necessary for Lucinda Elizabeth to housekeep on a small income. For in 1852 she married George Carr Shaw, Bernard Shaw's father, a willful and astonishing match which alienated her aunt, and which does not seem even to have had the excuse of being founded on personal attachment: although of this, at least in the form of a sudden romantic impulse, it is not possible to be really sure. The fact is Shaw's mother felt unhappy and restricted in her life with her aunt, and although George Shaw was a rather unlikely bachelor of forty, "with a squint and a vein of humour which delighted in anticlimax," as his son (who inherited the style of humor) puts it, he was unquestionably a way of escape. And his government pension of £60 a year probably seemed, to the ignorant girl of twenty-one, infinitely more than the pittance (even in those days) it undoubtedly was.

Mr. Shaw was also the part-owner of a corn mill, inadequately run in a disastrous partnership, and (although he hotly denied this when pressed by his tearful *fiancée,* who rashly believed him) he was far from the teetotaler his principles urged him to become. His son discovered this the hard way one day when his father, during a walk, pretended to throw him into the canal and very nearly succeeded. "When we got home I said to my mother as an awful and hardly credible discovery: 'Mamma: I think Papa is drunk.' This was too much for her. She replied 'When is he anything else?' "

The ill-assorted marriage was further encouraged by a sudden outbreak of that riotous family quarreling, verging on farce, which seems to afflict the Irish. In fact, Lucinda's father, Shaw's grandfather, chose this moment to remarry:

his choice being the penniless daughter of an old friend who was already deeply his debtor. Shaw's mother innocently mentioning this intention to her maternal uncle, a Kilkenny squire and lawyer to whom her father owed money, found herself the full butt of her father's rage when he was arrested for debt at the request of the squire on the actual morning of his wedding. The *imbroglio* sorted itself out, but the house of a new stepmother whose marriage had been so nearly thwarted can have seemed hardly more palatable to Lucinda than its only alternative, the house of her tyrannous aunt. She therefore married George Carr Shaw within one month of her father's own wedding: at St. Peter's Church, Dublin, on June 17, 1852.

In spite of some unlikely characteristics, Shaw brought to his son a heredity not entirely shapeless and unproductive. "My mother had no comedic impulses, and never uttered an epigram in her life: all my comedy is a Shavian inheritance," wrote Bernard. From the Shaws, too, he gained a background of Irish Protestant landed gentry, descending from a captain in the army of William of Orange who landed in Ireland in the late seventeenth century, and who was of English and Scottish blood. The Shaws' claim to be descended from the Macduff immortalized in Shakespeare's *Macbeth* has never been clearly substantiated.

His father Shaw described as being "of the downstart race of younger sons"; in fact the Shaws combined gentility with poverty in a depressing degree, and in Bernard's own lifetime moved only in an extreme outer orbit to a more glittering stellar cluster of richer and more distinguished Shaw relatives. The family seat of these was at Bushy Park near Rathfarnham, founded by a Sir Robert Shaw, who was a member for Dublin in the Imperial Parliament and who also founded the Royal Bank of Ireland—still known in young Bernard Shaw's time as Shaw's Bank. When Shaw was ten years old Bushy Park passed to a Sir Frederick Shaw, Recorder of Dublin and a member of the Imperial Parliament for Dublin itself and later Dublin University, Trinity College. A spattering of rebellious clergymen and lawyers also lined the family avenue, which as its greatest genius loomed on the scene took an abrupt descent both in social distinction and in revenue.

The effect on Shaw was embittering and to an extent survived into his later life, giving him in old age that sense of financial insecurity which one also often finds in successful actors who have never entirely recovered from the wretched circumstances of poverty and frequent unemployment in their early careers. "Be a tramp or be a millionaire: it matters little which: what does matter is being a poor relation of the rich; and that is the very devil," he wrote years later. "The adult who has been poor as a child, will never get the chill of poverty out of his bones."

"The way we were brought up, or rather not brought up, doesn't bear thinking of," he also wrote. Nevertheless, the Shavian sense of humor—which was also to a degree the Irish sense of humor, and equally the ironic sense of humor of Dickens—seems to have sustained the household and given it at times a kind of crazy *panache*. Shaw described his father's Irish mischief in the midst of the near-ruin of the corn mill firm of Clibborn and Shaw, due to the bankruptcy of a client. This catastrophe, which reduced Clibborn to tears, sent Shaw's father to the privacy of the warehouse for a burst of irrepressible laughter.

This sense of anticlimax, as his son points out, enriched his own comedy writing. And it is the basis of the imp that so surprised or shocked some English people, including Harley Granville-Barker who accompanied Shaw to his mother's funeral, at which Shaw resolutely refused to display the appropriate feeling; later describing in a letter to Mrs. Patrick Campbell the "wildly funny" ending to the episode when, looking down to the lower floor of the crematorium, they saw two attendants like cooks, tongs in hand, "deftly and busily picking nails and scraps of coffin handles out of Mama's dainty little heap of ashes and samples of bone. Mama herself being at that moment leaning over beside me shaking with laughter."

Shaw's earlier description of the scene in the cremation chamber after the service, in the same letter, tends to be overlooked; but it is a very different revelation of the writer.

> People are afraid to see it; but it is wonderful. . . . No heat. No noise. No roaring draught. No flame. No fuel. It looked cool, clean, sunny, though no sun could get there. You would have walked in or put your hand in without misgiving. Then the violet coffin moved again and went in, feet first. And behold! The feet burst miraculously into streaming ribbons of garnet coloured lovely flame, smokeless and eager, like pentecostal tongues, and as the whole coffin passed in it sprang into flame all over; and my mother became that beautiful fire.

It was the same enchanted sense of the beauty of flame—"the burning bush"—which had penetrated into the scenes between the artist Dubedat and his wife in *The Doctor's Dilemma* some years before; and Shaw in the first passage was up to the Irish trick of irreverent humor and anticlimax, always hard to understand for the unhumorous, who take sentimentality and exterior grief as the necessary pattern of human behavior, without being able to conceive of that resilient quickness of brain and humor that may mask a feeling equally deep, refusing to parade itself in public. Elsewhere, Shaw wrote: "My father, by the way, found something in a funeral which tickled his sense of humor; and this characteristic I have inherited. I never grieve; but I do not forget."

Shaw never wore his heart on his sleeve: a fact which misled many people to assume that he had no heart to wear. As regards his private generosities and kindnesses to those in difficulty or distress, we know that was not the case; and the episode of his mother's funeral gives us a startling but obviously genuine glimpse of a side of her that may well have been for a time a point of contact with Shaw's often amusing father, and held the marriage together in its earlier stages. If her son felt certain her ghost joined in his amusement at her funeral—"she would have enjoyed it immensely"—we may be sure he had grounds for his supposition, and the Shaw ménage of his childhood was not without its humorous interludes on the part of both parents.

It was in other ways a haphazard, bohemian family circle, wildly unsatisfactory to any earnest social worker of our own time, with the children (Lucy, Agnes and George Bernard, known as "Sonny," the youngest) delegated very largely to kitchen feeding and upbringing by servants and a governess, Miss Caroline Hill. Sonny, born on July 26, 1856, was at first the object of some affection and pride to his father, who recounted his childish progress in almost daily letters to the mother when she was away from home. And although St. John Ervine in his biography is harshly, almost vindictively, critical of Shaw's mother as a woman of cold, hard heart, unable to give love, and bitterly disillusioned in her feckless husband, Shaw's own picture of the unstable, ill-run home is a warmer one. He has pointed out her inadequacies from the "technical" point of view of a modern welfare worker (though adding that "her almost complete neglect of me had the advantage that I could idolize her to the utmost pitch of my imagination and had no sordid disillusioning contacts with her"); and he admits his father was impecunious and unsuccessful, and could do nothing that interested her. "Had there not been imagination, idealization, the charm of music, the charm of lovely seas and sunsets, and our natural kindness and gentleness, it is impossible to say what cynical barbarism we might not have grown into."

The reservations are interesting, for they point to a

harmony and freedom from strife or quarrel surprising in the circumstances, and explaining Shaw's own gentleness of manner, and total freedom from bad temper, in his personal relationships in later life—often commented on by his intimate friends, and disbelieved by those who never knew him and mistook the gay but critical thrusts of his pen for personal ill-humor.

The Shaw children were born in Dublin, and the reference to seas and sunsets needs explanation. "My mother's salvation came through music," wrote Shaw. She was, in fact, the possessor of a beautiful mezzo-soprano voice of great purity of tone, and if she neglected her household duties this personal gift was not one which it was in her nature to ignore. She therefore took lessons from George John Vandaleur Lee, an unconventional voice production teacher who was something of a "character" in Dublin. He was the author of a book on his singing method—*The Voice: Its Artistic Production, Development and Preservation* (1869)—and so efficient at his job (in a "Golden Age" of singers which nevertheless suffered, like our own, too often from the ruin of good voices through bad vocal training) that, as Shaw says, his mother's voice was preserved by his method "without a scrape on it" until her death at over eighty. Lee (though uninterested in any but vocal music) was also a conductor, and the *soirées* at the Shaw home under his direction became an absorbing feature of family life.

When Shaw was ten Lee's brother died, and by an apparently equable arrangement he came to live permanently with the Shaws, now residing at No. 1 Hatch Street, having left Synge Street where G.B.S. was born. It was Lee who bought Torca Cottage on Dalkey Hill, in the country outside Dublin and overlooking Dublin and Killiney Bays. With its strands of pure sand and its view of the Wicklow and Dublin mountains, it was an enchantment to the boy, hitherto confined to the shabby-genteel Dublin streets.

> Happiness is never my aim. Like Einstein I am not happy and do not want to be happy: I have neither time nor taste for such comas, attainable at the price of a pipeful of opium or a glass of whiskey, though I have experienced a very superior quality of it two or three times in dreams. But I had one moment of ecstatic happiness in my childhood when my mother told me that we were going to live in Dalkey. I had only to open my eyes there to see such pictures as no painter could make for me. I could not believe that such skies existed anywhere else in the world until I read Shakespear's "this majestical roof fretted with golden fire," and wondered where he could have seen it if not from Torca Cottage.
>
> The joy of it has remained with me all my life.

This experience of natural beauty Shaw counted a part of his education as vital as books, pictures, and music, the true sources of learning to him in his youth. His formal schooling at Wesley Connexial School on the South side of St. Stephen's Green, which he attended from the age of eleven, and later at the Central Model School and Dublin English Scientific and Commerical Day School, seems never to have deeply engaged his interest or notably widened his horizons. The Central Model, a largely Roman Catholic school, was for snobbish reasons considered outside the class of Episcopalians with aristocratic connections such as the Shaws, and Shaw as a boy was deeply humiliated by being sent there at Lee's suggestion. His sojourn was brief and fruitless. Latin he learned from a clerical uncle, and from another uncle, a ship's surgeon named Walter Gurly, he picked up, by proxy, a Rabelaisian experience of a very different kind of life. From this he emerged with the greater knowledge but unsullied outlook of that form of innocence which is essentially uncorruptible.

Yet in Dublin were laid, even before he left school at

fourteen, the foundations of a general culture of remarkable breadth, enabling him later to move at ease as a critic between the arts of painting and music as well as the drama. The National Gallery of Ireland was a deep educative force in his boyhood—"I believe I am the only Irishman who has ever been in it, except the officials," he quipped—and was augmented in London at the National Gallery in Trafalgar Square and at Hampton Court. And thanks partly to the influence of his mother and Lee, partly to his own insatiable thirst for knowledge and musical "ear," he claimed to know before the age of fifteen "at least one important work by Handel, Mozart, Beethoven, Mendelssohn, Rossini, Bellini, Donizetti, Verdi and Gounod from cover to cover." At sixteen he also began to study symphonic scores, and read all the musical scientific textbooks including Mozart's *Succinct Thoroughbass*—a "scrap of paper with some helpful tips on it which he scrawled for his pupil Sussmaier," wrote Shaw. Many years later Sir Edward Elgar told him it was "the only document in existence of the smallest use to a student composer."

His attempts to play these scores at the piano were enthusiastic but inefficient—a lack of accomplishment he shared with Wagner, also wholly self-taught—but his musical memory seems to have been photographic and his appreciative sense uncommonly sound as well as eclectic. When he turned to literature he read Shelley's works complete, and no writer in later life had a profounder knowledge and understanding of the true, mentally tough and strongly practical poet and reformer behind the popular myth of "ineffectual angel." The result was seen years later in Marchbanks in *Candida* and in many atheistic and political influences in other works by Shaw.

His religious background had been as indeterminate as almost all home contributions to his education except music. Officially Irish Protestant, "our family atmosphere," he wrote in *Sixteen Self Sketches*, "was one of derisive free-thinking. By the time I was ten years old my parents had given up even the respectable pretence of churchgoing; and I myself, after reasoning the step quite deliberately, had stopped saying my prayers on the ground that I was an atheist." But religious argument continued at home under the stimulus of Lee and his father, and his interest in the phenomenon and the mystery of life never left him, becoming transmuted into what he called "the Life Force" and a study of the Creative Evolution theories of Lamarck in particular. "Rationalism was also associated with Materialism," he wrote in *Sixteen Self Sketches,* in the chapter headed "What is my Religious Faith?", "and I was and still am a Vitalist to whom vitality, though the hardest of hard facts, is a complete mystery. I have to deal constantly in reason and with matter; but I am neither a Rationalist nor a Materialist."

The snobbery of his social English-Irish background, which looked down on the "native" Roman Catholics of slums and suburbs, soon evaporated when his mother and Lee, forced to ignore convention in order to get the best musical performance, invited Catholics and indeed all classes to the choral sessions at the house, and the young Shaw was quick to note that a strangely indiscriminate Providence had given to the despised Catholics most of the best voices!

In fact, he could learn only when his interest was engaged, and then he absorbed knowledge like a sponge, never to be squeezed and sucked dry again. His retention of knowledge was phenomenal to his death at the age of ninety-four. When he left school and, owing to some family influence, entered the Dublin estate office of Charles Uniacke and Thomas Courtney Townshend as a junior clerk, at a salary of eighteen shillings a month, his horizons outside the office continued to expand. Among the friends who had a lasting influence on him was Chichester Bell, a cousin of Graham Bell who invented the telephone and a nephew of Melville Bell, inventor of a phonetic script, Visible Speech. Phonetics remained a fascinated hobby for him, its effects immortalized in Professor Higgins of *Pygmalion* (or as some now prefer to call it, *My Fair Lady*); and to the promotion of its subsidiary science of a reformed alphabet Shaw left a large proportion of his fortune on his death.

It was Chichester Bell also who first introduced Shaw seriously to the "new music" of Wagner, which he had up to then known only through the Grand March in *Tannhäuser*, performed with chilling lack of distinction by a military band. Shaw bought a score of *Lohengrin* and studied it: "the first few bars completely converted me," he wrotc, and *The Perfect Wagnerite* sprang years later from this first flame of recognition of a new genius and prophet, to be honored and defended from calumny and public ignorance (like all—the rare—great critics, Shaw was a born crusader, and a denigrator only of the genuinely mediocre).

Shaw remained in his uncongenial office work for a period of five years. He hated the work itself, although clever enough to rise quickly to a senior position, carrying responsibility far beyond the capacity of the normal boy of his years. His experience of rent collecting in this firm provided material for his first play, *Widowers' Houses*.

In the meantime there had been a vital upheaval in the home in Hatch Street. Lee's book on voice production had proved such a success—including an edition in England—that the teacher's spirit was aroused to further conquests, and in 1872 he departed for London. As he had been teaching Lucy, Shaw's sister, who had a fine soprano voice, and Mrs. Shaw had ambitions for her daughter as a prima donna, she decided to make the break with her husband and follow Lee to England. It was partly because of this imminent crisis that Bernard,[2] in 1871, had been withdrawn from school and placed in, if hardly profitable, at least remunerated employment.

The Shaws in fact had to face a threatened loss of income owing to Lee's departure, for he had long helped to sustain the home; and Mrs. Shaw's main objective was work as a music teacher in London, with Lee—who had set up a fashionable practice in Park Lane—to help her find pupils. Shaw himself scoffed at suggestions—notably by the incurable womaniser Frank Harris in his Shaw biography—that Lee was in fact his mother's lover. "My mother could have boarded and lodged the three musketeers and D'Artagnan for twenty years without discovering their sex; and they would no more have obtruded it on her than they would have ventured to smoke in her drawing-room." His own continence in this respect makes this assertion not unlikely: again we sense hereditary roots.

Shaw's father, from his slender means, provided his errant wife with £1 a week until his death, and removed with his son to lodgings in Harcourt Street. Here they remained until 1876, the year of the death of Shaw's sister Agnes from consumption and his own departure, by choice, from Ireland and the estate office.

He was twenty years of age. He had vaguely wished to be a painter or an opera singer; but, as he has said, he had never felt inclined to write, any more than to breathe. England lay before him across the Channel, holding the secret of an uncharted future.

[2] He disliked the name George, and dropped it by choice for professional purposes.

Chapter 2

London, Politics and Marriage

A PHOTOGRAPH published by Shaw in *Sixteen Self Sketches* shows him at the time he first came to London: beneath it the master dramatist of ninety-three has inscribed: "Immature, and apparently an arrant prig." There are only the scruffy beginnings of a beard; the eyes are as unaccountably serious as the center hair-parting; the lips are curiously supercilious; and there is proof, if any were needed, that for whatever reason Shaw grew the famous beard, it was not—as often in vain men—to hide a chin of receding weakness. In fact he has his mother's chin: firm and rather square, matching in determination the singularly direct gaze of the eyes.

In later life Shaw very rarely allowed himself to be photographed without an elfin twinkle, giving an effect of Mephistophelean mischief to sustain the public figure he frankly referred to as "that brilliant fiction known as G.B.S." But here was the original face behind the mask of the clown and sage, so carefully cultivated to match both the witty prose style and, as the years passed, the accepted prophet behind the pen. It was a personality not fully developed yet perhaps never quite lost; for if the glitter of humor played such glancing lights about the latent prig that he seemed to vanish from view, it is nevertheless true that buffoonery, and even Irish charm, were in the nature of mirages thrown up by Shaw to mask an innate shyness, and to water the arid deserts of the messages he had to convey. It was by his wit and his gift of entertaining, the gift of laughter, that he got people to listen in the public lecture hall, in the press, and later in the theatre; for like Gilbert and Gilbert's Jack Point, he knew that "he who'd make his fellow creatures wise, must always gild the philosophic pill."

The humor, of course, was *in* him; it is not something that can be invented and sustained. But the man and the message beneath the humor were deadly serious, and to forget this is to dilute the essence of Shaw and vastly underestimate his importance.

He had no immediate visions of taking London by storm. "I left Ireland because I had no apparent future there; for in the interval between Lee's emigration and the literary and dramatic revival led by W. B. Yeats and Lady Gregory Dublin was an art Sahara." It was thirty years before he revisited the country, and his feelings about Ireland and the Irish remained, for a writer of such steady views and clear thought, strangely flexible, fluctuating between an apparent hatred (especially of Dublin) and a hereditary pride which included not only the skies of Dalkey, fretted golden fire to his Celtic imagination, but also his Irish blood.

A paragraph he wrote in the third person in a guide to his biographer, Frank Harris, as to the way his life should actually have been written, is revealing of this schism between his English and Irish "pull":

> Shaw was full not only of Ibsen, but of Wagner, of Beethoven, of Goethe, and, curiously, of John Bunyan. The English way of being great by flashes: Shakespear's way, Ruskin's way, Chesterton's way, without ever following the inspiration upon which William Morris put his finger when he said that Ruskin could say the most splendid things and forget them five minutes after, could not disguise its incoherence from an Irishman. "The Irish," he says, "with all their detestable characteristics, are at least grown up. They think systematically: they dont stop in the middle of a game of golf to admire a grandeur of thought as if it were a sunset, and then turn back to their

game as the really serious business of their life." His native pride in being Irish persists in spite of his whole adult career in England and his preference for English and Scottish friends.

It was, of course, the fecklessness of the Irish—the "detestable characteristics" which doubtless included in Shaw's mind his father's drinking habits and the improvidence of many of his relatives—that disturbed the puritan and thinker in Shaw, and for all his Irish humor and "gift of the gab" gave him in his own country a sense of being odd man out, so that he had none of the emigrant's nostalgia to return. He was certainly not wholly understood by the English, either; but his lasting friendships, political and artistic, were all made in England, for it was only there that he reached the position where he could mingle with the best people—using "best" in its intellectual sense—find minds of bright, congenial metal on which to strike the sharp blade of his wit and thought (like Wagner's *Nothung* to Siegfried, so needful a weapon to Shaw), and create and criticize in a metropolitan limelight essential both to his personality and the propagation of his ideas.

Yet of the father left alone in Ireland—where he died in a placid old age, having achieved at last a lifelong ambition to become and remain a teetotaler—Shaw could look back, in 1919, with tolerance and something like affection. "I believe," he wrote, "it was the happiest time of his life. No more Lee, no more wife, no more grown-up children. Towards the end, one or two newspaper cuttings and reviews convinced him that his son was going to achieve his father's somehow missed destiny and be 'a great man' . . . He was really, as men go, humane and likeable . . . He was full of self-reproaches and humiliations when he was not full of secret jokes, and was either biting his moustache and whispering deepdrawn damns, or shaking with silent paroxysms of laughter. His partner in business was comparatively rough mannered; and my father believed that the little tacts and kindlinesses and genialities with which he allayed the susceptibilities hurt by his partner kept the business alive. They certainly helped."

He gives, too, a sketch of his mother at odds with Ervine's bitter picture, suggesting that his own occasional expressed horror of his early upbringing did not reflect on her good nature: ". . . as it happens, my mother was also very kind, incapable of striking a child or an animal, hating to see a flower thrown away or picked to pieces. Many women with her provocation would have hated my father: she was not in the least bitter about him. She had no respect for him in the common sense of the word, as he could do nothing dramatically interesting or effective; but she took him as he was, in the kindly Irish fashion, without trumping up a moral case against him or blaming him. We were all like that, more or less: his position in the household was just what he was capable of taking: he was Papa in the fullest sense always; and the dynamic Lee got none of the affection Papa inspired."

It was, indeed, to his mother alone that Shaw must look for a home, so it was fortunate their tempers were both equable, for it was to be a number of years before Sonny was able to contribute his full share to the household expenses in London. If there was no strong bond of affection with his mother—who was most attached to the girl who died, Agnes, and more immediately interested in the budding career of her remaining daughter Lucy—there was some respect; she was not a demonstrative woman, and Shaw himself inherited her restraint.

Lee soon artistically proved a broken reed. London social conditions, according to Shaw, forced him into abandoning his singing "Method" in order to earn a good living "pretending to enable his pupils to sing like Patti in twelve lessons": upon which Shaw's mother, whose iron integrity matched her son's, abandoned him in spite of her continuing hopes for Lucy's singing future. She became music instructress at North London College, with such success that she was in continuous demand as teacher and singer by other schools and groups until she retired in old age, when Shaw's earnings made this possible.

Lucy's career, mainly in light opera, never fulfilled all the hopes her beautiful voice had aroused, especially when she had sung the florid part of Amina in *La Sonnambula* in Dublin in one of Lee's amateur productions. She lacked her brother's temperament and professional outlook as an actress, although according to him "it cost her no effort to sing or play anything she had once heard, or to read any music at sight," and when the tenor in *La Sonnambula* lost his place and his head she "obligingly sang most of his part as well as her own." Her good looks and charm were sufficient to win her many admirers, among them Oscar Wilde and his brother Willie, both said by Shaw to have been in love with her in Ireland (Shaw first met Oscar Wilde through his sister). In middle life she married a tenor in the same company as herself, but as he gambled and was overfond of women she left him, divorcing him after a long period and reverting to her maiden name. Then came what Shaw describes as "the Shavian touch." "Later on he turned up again, lonely and at a loss for somewhere to spend his evenings. Lucy immediately tolerated him as a waif and stray, though as a husband she had found him unbearable. So he became her frequent visitor until he died . . ."

"She broke many hearts, but never her own," wrote her brother, though with what certainty is doubtful, as they were later so much apart. Like her mother, she seems to have been rather cold and reserved, and was perhaps a little jealous of her brother. She published one or two magazine stories, and one book purporting to be letters by an old woman advising a young one, so cynical that it shocked not only her mother but almost Shaw himself. There seems to have been no great bond of affection between brother and sister; yet Shaw was with her when she died, and probably he gave her the copy of *The Perfect Wagnerite* now in my possession which is inscribed in her handwriting: "Lucy Carr Shaw. March, 1899."

The next few years were entirely nebulous in Shaw's career. His mother gave him a home, "but there was hardly a word between us," he wrote. "She was a disillusioned woman." Yet she seems to have accepted—even if Lucy always did not—the fact that her only son had some right to his share in the household supported mainly by her earnings as a music teacher. His first tentative jobs petered out and eventually he settled down openly to unsuccessful authorship and journalism, writing articles which were either rejected outright, or for which he was frequently unpaid or ill-paid. His work also included "ghosting" for Lee as music critic on an unimportant journal called *The Hornet,* which ceased publication in October, 1877.

Between 1880 and 1883, he wrote five novels—*Immaturity, The Irrational Knot, An Unsocial Socialist, Cashel Byron's Profession* and *Love Among the Artists*—all of which failed to find a publisher, although they were the product of typical Shavian industry (he conscientiously filled five pages of a penny exercise book every morning, in addition to other writing and political work). They contained a great deal of the early ferment of sociological, artistic and political ideas which were to mature in his later plays and pamphlets. When it was published years later, after Shaw's success in other fields, *Cashel Byron's Profession* rather unexpectedly enchanted Robert Louis Stevenson, who read it in Samoa. But in a preface to the first edition of *Immaturity,* published fifty years after it was written, Shaw gives a disturbing and comic-pathetic glimpse of his own appalling poverty at this time, borne out also in a letter to Ellen Terry: "Up to the time I was 29, actually twenty-nine, I was too shabby for any woman to tolerate me. I stalked about in a decaying green coat, cuffs trimmed with the scissors, terrible boots, and so on."

Yet in spite of his dejection at these rejections of his novels (when the fifth shared the fate of the other four, he abandoned the sixth he was then writing, and the novelist's craft for ever), he had by now a hard inner core of determination and self-knowledge which could not be deflected. And his integrity remained untouched. He would rather be anything, he wrote, than a literary "hack," and in his whole life he never debased his pen to mere potboiling. He was a rebel with a succession of causes, his brief despairs warmed by an irrepressible sun of Irish humor, and his natural asceticism sustaining his fortitude. In his poverty he was aided, too, by those communistic free shelters to the book and art lover, the British Museum Reading Room and the National Gallery, whose value to him in these years he never forgot (many of his MSS and other Shaw materials have now gone to the British Museum to form a large collection there).

His earnings, even when his name became better known in the literary reviews, were for long small. As late as 1889, at the age of thirty-three, his total year's earnings were only £197 6s. 10d., a great deal of his work for his chosen causes, including all his political lecturing, being unpaid, sometimes at his own insistence. Without his mother's home and food he certainly could not have survived, though he has often been blamed for taking her help by those always ready to believe a great artist's work is expendable, or could at least have been achieved simultaneously with more prosaic methods of earning a living. There is no indication, fortunately, that his mother, who herself was devoted to the art of music, shared this view, and her forbearance, if it was no more, of her financially unsatisfactory son reaped its reward in later years, when he provided for her liberally.

In the meantime he worked with undeviating intensity,

sure now that his future lay in the field of writing: but writing always with a purpose. And rapidly he was accumulating the amazingly varied fund of knowledge that was to be a keynote of his genius, and mark him out for versatility and virtuosity even in an age not yet prone to suffocate the free range of its talent in the iron bands of "specialization," as our own has done. A brilliant mind eager for knowledge, like Shaw's, can explore many fields of art and thought and extract the essential core of all of them without superficiality on the one hand or dry pedantry on the other; and it will excel at criticism because all the matters of life and art are interrelated to an extent, and knowledge in one will help broaden knowledge in another in a way impossible where such range of understanding does not exist. Much of the poverty of criticism in our time springs from lack of this breadth of experience and vision, and creatively writers themselves are the worse for it.

Shaw's work as a critic—the most stimulating of the past century—of music and the theatre falls into the scope of the next chapters, when his final and most important bent, as a writer for the theatre, begins to crystallize. But simultaneously his interests were concentrating more and more on social problems and politics, something largely unprepared for in Ireland where his passion for music and painting outweighed anything else, including his love for the theatre. But he had seen Barry Sullivan and Henry Irving act at the Gaiety Theatre, Dublin, and had been particularly impressed by Irving, whom he named of the two "his man." And it was in Ireland, nevertheless, that the seed was sown of his lifelong loathing of poverty and urge to eradicate it. This was when a servant, instead of taking him for walks by the canal as she had been ordered, took him instead to visit her friends in the most squalid of Dublin slums. These slums struck a horror in him that he never forgot.

He brought from Ireland, where he had a few close

friends, a painful shyness in society at large, for which, with no "small talk" in his repertoire and a dislike of genteel shams, he was in any case unfitted, quite apart from the poverty of his appearance. He walked enormously long distances (a habit that was to persist until nearly his ninetieth year), and explored everything London had to offer in the way of concert halls, art galleries and museums: an attenuated, Dickensian scarecrow with frayed sleeves and an incongruous battered tall hat, his hair, beard and eyebrows with but a shadow of the Mephistophelean upward twitch that was to keep artists and sculptors busy across a span of nearly half a century. ("It is impossible to move without coming up against Shaw in effigy," wrote his friend H. G. Wells in humorous and jealous disgust; and it is worth noting that Shaw himself explained in old age, "My auburn hair was never really Highland red like my sister Agnes's . . . I was a 'blonde beast' of Danish type unmistakeably.")

What finally broke down his reserve and launched him into political life was a chance visit to a debating society called the Zetetical, where in the winter of 1879 he was taken by a friend, James Lecky, an exchequer clerk from Ireland privately interested in phonetics and keyboard music. If Shaw often chose friends not professionally involved in the arts, they were never amateur in the less knowledgeable sense of the word: Lecky in fact contributed an article on systems of tuning keyed instruments to the first edition of Sir George Grove's *Dictionary of Music.*

The Zetetical, wrote Shaw in *Sixteen Self Sketches,* was

> a junior copy of the once well-known Dialectical Society founded to discuss John Stuart Mill's *Essay on Liberty* when that was new. Both societies were strongly Millite. In both there was complete freedom of discussion, political, religious and sexual. Women took an important part in the debates, a special feature of which was that each speaker, at the conclusion of his speech, could be cross-examined on it. The tone

was strongly individualistic, atheistic, Malthusian, Ingersollian, Darwinian, and Herbert Spencerian. Huxley, Tyndall, and George Eliot were on the shelves of all the members. Championship of the Married Women's Property Act had hardly been silenced even by the Act itself . . . and no words were too strong for invective against such leading cases as those of Annie Besant and Shelley, whose children were torn from them by the Lord Chancellor because, as professed atheists, they were presumed to be unfit for parentage. Socialism was regarded as an exploded fallacy of Robert Owen's; and nobody dreamt that within five years Marxist Socialism would snatch away all the younger generation, and sweep the Dialectical and Zetetical Societies into the blind cave of eternal night.

When I went with Lecky to the Zetetical meeting I had never spoken in public. I knew nothing about public meetings or their order. I had an air of impudence, but was really an arrant coward, nervous and self-conscious to a heartbreaking degree. Yet I could not hold my tongue. I started up and said something in the debate, and then, feeling that I had made a fool of myself, as in fact I had, I was so ashamed that I vowed I would join the Society; go every week; speak in every debate; and become a speaker or perish in the attempt.

He carried out this resolution, though he maintained he "suffered agonies that no one suspected," and soon was moving out so freely in other directions—in public debates following lectures, in the streets, in the parks, at demonstrations, "anywhere and everywhere possible"—that it is obvious fear had given way to exhilaration. This does not, of course, mean that he ever conquered his nerves before launching into a speech: like all great speakers he was as temperamental as an actor in this respect. But that passionate self-exhibitionism which was yet at the same time a passionate desire to redress public ills, and right a world un-Shavianly wrong-headed, had taken hold of him in a grip that could never, to his ninety-fifth year, let go.

He had succumbed, as his audiences everywhere succumbed, to the lilt of his Irish brogue, his lightning wit, and above all that pearl beyond price to the orator, originality of mind and phrasing. ". . . though ignorant of economics, I had read, in my boyhood, Mill on Liberty, on Representative Government, and on the Irish Land Question; and I was as full of Darwin, Tyndall, and George Eliot as most of my audience. Yet every subject struck my mind at an angle that produced reflections new to my audience."

His ignorance of economics was redressed after he ventured to speak at a meeting of Hyndman's Marxist Democratic Federation, and blazoned the doctrine of the American Land and Tax reformist Henry George, whom he had recently heard lecture. He was contemptuously dismissed as a novice who had not yet read the great first volume of Marx's *Capital*; upon which he promptly read it, and returned to announce his complete conversion. "Immediately," wrote Shaw, "contempt changed to awe; for Hyndman's disciples had not read the book themselves, it being then accessible only in Deville's French version in the British Museum Reading Room, my daily resort."

But the Marxist Democratic Federation was an organization largely composed of manual workers, and the Fabian Society, newly formed in January, 1884, offered a more congenial setting for Shaw, being a body of educated middle-class intelligentsia. The Society was the stepping-stone to the first English Independent Labour Party, whose first member to be elected to the House of Commons was Keir Hardie, representing the constituency of West Ham, in 1892. Shaw drafted with Hardie its first party program, having seven months previously published a *Labour Manifesto* of his own for the Fabian Society, among many other tracts written wholly by himself or in collaboration.

The irony of the position of moneyed intellectuals—as well as poverty-stricken ones like Shaw—in the groups and parties of social reform, persists today and is a consistent cause of internal irruption; for the fact remains the British public as a whole fears, distrusts and dislikes culture and intellectuals, and the growing power today of Trade Unionism—in a few instances—as a form of proletariat dictatorship would have disturbed the original Fabians as it began to disturb Shaw before his death. For although radical organizations such as the Fabian Society were founded on the assumption that mass education of the workers would not only sweep away social ills, but enable working class people to employ their leisure enjoying a culture until that time restricted to the rich, the improvement in conditions of life has, in fact, produced no comparable rise in mental equipment or artistic taste; so that in 1960 a young working-class playwright, Mr. Arnold Wesker, was still actively engaged in trying to arouse a Trade Union sense of responsibility in art education and support.

It was his later realization of this, long after the battle for working-class representation in the House of Commons had been won, that forced Shaw to face the fact that government needed something more than democracy reduced to its strictest and most impartial terms: "To make democracy work you must have an aristocratic democracy." It led him in the thirties into an apparent leaning towards at least partial dictatorship as a solution, though he had little sympathy with Hitler or Mussolini as such (he guyed them mercilessly in his play *Geneva,* while as a born debater and dramatist giving them a few good arguments to be demolished).

His ideal of benevolent government by a political "aristocracy" has to some extent to be observed in all democracies; the man of ability will always be needed to pass the laws and undertake the responsibilities of office. Shaw's first belief in Marxism as a solution underwent a change as he himself grew in experience and political knowledge;

his was too shrewd and wide-ranging a brain ever to remain inflexible to new impressions and ideas. In essentials, as he protested to Winston Churchill, he remained a Marxist; but with Philip Wicksteed and Sidney Webb as mentors he came to realize that Marx was not valid on capitalist political economy or on the law of rent—partly because of his lack of administrative experience and of personal contacts in English society while he lived here.

Webb's prophet was John Stuart Mill, particularly in Mill's socialistic phase, and Shaw's friendship with Webb dated at least from the birth of the Fabian Society, of which Webb was a main architect. It was to continue in deep intimacy until Webb's death, as Lord Passfield. In 1946, Webb was still, though near his deathbed, able to contribute briefly and movingly to the tributes to Shaw on his ninetieth birthday, gathered together by Stephen Winten in the volume, *G.B.S. 90*.

"I travelled with him in many parts of England, France, Belgium, Holland and Germany. Everywhere I gained something. Now after sixty years my memory fails me."

Webb was in some ways Shaw's antithesis: a small gnomelike man with a vast brain for figures revealed in the disproportionate size of his head, methodical to the point of dullness as a politician. Although he became Colonial Secretary in the Labour Government of 1930, he was without that electric flare of imagination and personality Shaw possessed in abundance, and thus escaped the political eminence often achieved by less able men. But combined with Shaw and later his brilliant wife Beatrice—who worshiped her husband with a possessiveness unusual in so intellectual a woman, and who never liked or trusted the uncontrollable Puck in Shaw—his capacity was a major factor in the promulgation of Socialism through the Fabian Society and Labour Party, as well as through the monumental books he wrote with his wife.

Shaw too took his part in this literary activity: *Fabian*

Essays, published in 1889 under his editorship, brought together essays on Socialism by seven of the most brilliant of the Society's members, including Webb, Mrs. Annie Besant, Sydney Olivier and Graham Wallas. And throughout his life he continued to read Webb's scripts, advising and rewriting where necessary: one of the many heavy labors without pay he was accustomed to take when a good cause, or a friend's need, were involved.

"Webb was all-of-one-piece," wrote Shaw, whose own prismatic brain and personality, reflecting lights in all directions, made him perhaps the more appreciative of this balanced oneness in others: "a man of extraordinary ability and equally extraordinary simplicity. Asquith described him as a saint. Without him I might have been a mere literary wisecracker, like Carlyle and Ruskin . . . . The difference between Shaw with Webb's brains, knowledge and official experience and Shaw by himself was enormous. But as I was and am an incorrigible histrionic mountebank, and Webb was the simplest of geniuses, I was often in the centre of the stage whilst he was invisible in the prompter's box."

This generous tribute leaves out of the picture—as Shaw presenting himself in his favorite public disguise was wont to do, to the great help of his detractors—the amount of indefatigable hard backroom work put in by Shaw in this as in all his enterprises. There is no doubt in addition that his *flair* for good relations—born of the instinct for "kindlinesses and genialities" he inherited from his father—and ready wit were valuable factors in holding together the strong and often divided temperaments that comprised the Fabian Cabinet.

> Whenever there was a quarrel I betrayed everybody's confidence by analyzing it and stating it lucidly in the most exaggerated terms. Result: both sides agreed that it was all my fault. I was denounced on all hands as a reckless mischief-maker, but forgiven as a privileged Irish lunatic.

I flatter myself that the unique survival of the Fabian Society among the forgotten wrecks of its rivals, all very contemptuous of it, was due not only to its policy, but in its early days to the one Irish element in its management.

The effect, on the receptive mind of a genius like Shaw, of the associations formed in a Society of this kind must be incalculable. The Fabian Society was of a limited membership—originally 150—totally out of proportion to its eventual influence on politics and society, and in it economic minds such as those of the Webbs and Sydney Olivier[1] were jostled against those of feminist firebrands such as Mrs. Besant, who later turned to Eastern mysticism and helped found the Theosophist Society, and of writers like H. G. Wells, science fiction novelist (as we would call it today), biologist and political author who remained a lasting, but, by temperament, often ticklish friend of Shaw's. The influences, of course, worked both ways; Shaw's work throughout his life carried echoes of his early Fabian associations (as late as 1936 *The Millionairess* contained a scene obviously—and anachronistically—inspired by Beatrice Webb's experience in a women's sweatshop when she was studying sociology the hard way as a girl), and his own multitudinous interests seeped inevitably into the consciousness of his friends. It is even a possibility, as I pointed out in a lecture to the Shaw Society,[2] that Wells' imagination was fired by Shaw's description of the Nibelungs' underground society in *The Ring*—a parallel, he believed, to the slave labor of early Victorian mines and factories—in his book *The Perfect Wagnerite,* which as a friend and fellow Fabian he probably read. "The Morlocks in his science-fantasy, *The Time Machine,* live underground much like the Nibelungen, as do the moon-dwellers in *The First*

[1] Olivier died a peer in 1943. Shaw had first met him in a body called the Land Reform Union, advocating Land Nationalization.
[2] Later published in article form in *Music Review* (August, 1958) under the title "Wagner and Shaw: a Dramatic Comparison."

Men in the Moon, and it may not be stretching reason too far to wonder if *The Invisible Man* owed anything, in its original idea, to the Tarnhelm." (The Tarnhelm was the magic helmet forged by the Nibelung smith Mime to render his brother Alberich invisible or enable him to change his form at will, thus aiding him to achieve supreme power as owner of the Rhinegold and enslaver of his people.)

It was through his political work, too, that Shaw came in contact with William Morris, socialist, poet, revolutionary designer, and progenitor, with Edward Burne-Jones, James Whistler, Dante Gabriel Rossetti and Algernon Swinburne, of the "aesthetic" movement in art and literature of the eighties. W. S. Gilbert had burlesqued the movement—or, rather, its excesses through disciples of Swinburne and Oscar Wilde—in his comic opera *Patience,* produced at the Opéra-Comique in April, 1881; but Morris himself was a highly practical artist whose printing and bookbinding experiments at Kelmscott appealed to Shaw, equally practical in all his artistic or social endeavors. His deep regard for Morris and his work and outlook was shown movingly on Morris' death, when he wrote: "You can lose a man like that by your own death, but not by his."

Wilde himself Shaw met only a few times and never on terms of intimacy; although by a curious chance Shaw's father had been operated upon for his squint by Wilde's father, the famous surgeon Sir William Wilde; the result being, according to Shaw (whose love of a good joke, as well as his father's photograph in old age, bring his *finale* under suspicion), that his father merely squinted in the opposite direction for the rest of his life! Oscar and Shaw had little in common as men or artists, still less as frequenters of two entirely opposed grades of society; and it is strange to find Shaw ranking *The Importance of Being Earnest,* that brilliant and immortal farce, far below Wilde's other plays, on the grounds that it was "heartless"—"the play, though extremely funny, was essentially hateful."

Strangely, too, he admired the other plays, which have certainly not worn well and seem now, in some ways, sentimental, Victorian and artificially melodramatic.

Shaw's innate chivalry and kindness made him rally to Wilde's defense, and even start an abortive attempt to get signatures asking for his release, when Wilde's tragedy overtook him. "My impulse to rally to him in his misfortune, and my disgust at 'the man Wilde' scurrilities of the newspapers, was irresistible," he wrote to Frank Harris. "I don't quite know why; for my charity to his perversion, and my recognition of the fact that it does not imply any general depravity or coarseness of character, came to me through reading and observation, not through sympathy. I have all the normal violent repugnance to homosexuality —if it be really normal, which nowadays [i.e. 1918] one is sometimes provoked to doubt."

Wilde's was not the only Victorian trial which inspired Shaw to rally to the defense of the accused. When the well-known editor, W. J. Stead, wrote a series of articles exposing the traffic in girl-children, sold by their poverty-stricken parents, and admitting he had "bought" a thirteen-year-old girl for £5 to prove his case, he was arrested and tried for abducting the girl. In the subsequent scandal his paper, *The Pall Mall Gazette* (for which Shaw wrote), was refused by the London bookstalls, and Shaw was among those who sold it on the streets during the trial.

By far the most important result to his private life of his socialist activities was his meeting with Charlotte Payne-Townshend, who on June 1, 1898, became his wife. She was born in County Cork in 1857, the daughter of an Irish barrister and an heiress to a fortune on her mother's side. Her wealth attracted the Webbs, who first met her in 1895—for it was an urgent need of the Fabians to attract rich converts to help propagate their work, and no bones were made about marrying off their poorer members, where the opportunity presented itself, to women able to meet this need. In fact, they seem to have had some original idea of marrying Charlotte to Graham Wallas, although it was obvious that marriage had not been especially attractive to Charlotte, then nearly forty, for her wealth must certainly have attracted suitors in the past. She was, moreover, passably good-looking in a rather elfin Irish way, her green eyes a notable feature in a broad but piquant face.

For her times and class, she was certainly social-minded. "By temperament," wrote Beatrice Webb in *Our Partnership,* "she is an anarchist, feeling any regulation or rule intolerable, a tendency which has been exaggerated by irresponsible wealth. She is romantic, but thinks herself cynical." Beatrice had some shrewdness in this matter of romanticism masked by an appearance of hard-headed practicability: Shaw, who "some people would call a cynic," had already himself been classed by her as "really an idealist of the purest water."

Shaw and Charlotte met first in August, 1896, although Beatrice had invited him earlier in the year to a Fabian "At Home" in the London School of Economics. This was at 10 Adelphi Terrace, where Charlotte had also taken a flat after donating £1,000 to the School Library and founding a woman's scholarship. This engagement he refused; but in August accepted an invitation to join the Webbs and Charlotte for six weeks in the rectory of Stratford St. Andrew, near Saxmundham, in Suffolk, which they had rented jointly for the summer. The friendship blossomed, although unexpectedly on Shaw's part, for he had not before seriously considered marriage; and despite the fact that he was now, with the production of several plays behind him, far better off financially (his income in 1896 reached £1,000 for the first time), he had a strong and independent aversion to seeming to marry for money. This delayed his decision for a considerable time.

An accident, and a sudden spur of initiative on Charlotte's part, in the end precipitated the marriage. Shaw's doubts had included some about Charlotte's own feelings, which he had communicated to Ellen Terry, with whom he was already in voluminous correspondence although they had never met. But his attraction was obvious to Ellen's love-experienced and friendly eyes, and in April, 1898, his resistance collapsed before a breakdown brought on by overwork. A slight injury to his foot developed into necrosis of the bone, involving two operations, and he was on crutches for eighteen months. At first news of the injury Charlotte, who had reached Rome on a proposed world tour with the Webbs, rushed back to London, and seeing the conditions under which G.B.S. was living in Fitzroy Square at once insisted he should be removed to her house in the country, at Haslemere in Surrey.

There was no alternative, and Shaw accepted the fact. They were married at the Register Office in the Strand, London, with the Fabians Graham Wallas and Henry Salt as witnesses.

Both were over forty, and they were in many ways ideally suited—even Charlotte's dislike of publicity balancing not unpleasantly for him Shaw's own irresistible genius to attract it. The marriage provided a long comradeship which grew in genuine devotion, so that when she died as an octogenarian Shaw, who had felt or declared himself fundamentally independent of others, was shaken to a degree that distressed his friends, and never really rallied from his loneliness at her loss.

Yet it was, if we are to believe his friend and biographer St. John Ervine, an entirely celibate union, not from Shaw's own continence in this respect, but from Charlotte's. Her rigid attitude about this, which in one revealing moment to Ervine Shaw said he thought he should have attempted to break down (he was gentle and never self-assertive where his affection was given), in no way affected her love for him, which was all-absorbing to the point of possessiveness and obvious to all their friends. (It is possibly psychologically true that the one lack stimulated it in other directions.) Nor, by his nature, did it reduce his respect for or loyalty to her. He had had his experience —though by some men's standards it was not large—of sex in relationships; though he was restrained or continent enough (he also put it down to his poverty, making him shy of women) not to have begun it until the age of twenty-nine, when he had a first violently disruptive and tempestuous affair with a young widow, Mrs. Jenny Paterson, which dragged on for several years owing partly to his natural kindness and inability to shake free of her. She was the original of Blanche Sartorius in *Widowers' Houses* and of Julia Craven in *The Philanderer;* and it is obvious he looked on the experience as one essential to the future dramatist.

"I was an absolute novice: I did not take the initiative in the matter," he wrote later; but her warmth of temperament, backed by an intelligence which added to her charm, opened new horizons to him which were inevitably of value to him as a writer for the theatre—all the more so because temperamentally passion was an element in life and human nature which he could not gauge fully out of his own character. On the other hand, although abstemious, he was a perfectly normal man and he admits susceptible; and it became clear, as his poverty and misgivings evaporated, that he had an irresistible Irish charm for women ("I did not pursue women: I was pursued by them").

He was able in most cases—as indeed many of the intellectual class of women he most frequently met were able to do—to keep the friendships on a platonic plane. There were a few other affairs, none serious or lasting on either side, and his platonic conquests are believed to include Annie Besant and Morris' daughter May, who turned the *affair* Shaw to comedy—and as near his discomfiture as a woman was likely to find possible—by marrying someone else while he was still basking in the confidence that there was a mutual and rather mystic unspoken "engagement" between them. His friendship with Florence Farr, the actress who created the part of Blanche Sartorius at the Royalty Theatre in 1892, and Janet Achurch, the Nora in the first English production of Ibsen's *A Doll's House* and later well-known in Shaw's plays, also hovered on, and perhaps overstepped, an intellectual-romantic borderline.

The truth is that Shaw had an unusually clear perception of the difference between love (or as he instinctively referred to it, marriage) and sex, and was able to keep the latter well in leash once he had had his experience of the disadvantages, as well as the advantages, of the purely physical *liaison*.

"The sex relation is not a personal relation," he wrote to Frank Harris, a buccaneer quite out of his depth with Shaw's private life in this respect. "It can be irresistibly desired and rapturously consummated between persons who could not endure one another for a day in any other relation. If I were to tell you every such adventure I have enjoyed you would be none the wiser as to the sort of man I am."

"As man and wife," he added of himself and Charlotte, "we found a relation in which sex had no part. It ended the old gallantries, flirtations and philanderings for both of us. Even of these it was the ones that were never consummated that left the longest and kindliest memories." He gives, too, a hint that in part this relationship was because Charlotte feared she was beyond the age safely to bear a child. She had, indeed, no wish for children, being the kind of woman—they are more than is generally realized—to whom love of her chosen man was fully sufficient and undivided. She was, in fact, in spite of her inhibitions (and presumably one must believe Shaw in this), both devoted to him and at times deeply jealous of his friendships. Such marriages are not unknown and often far from unhappy, especially where the man has himself a need for a part-maternal relationship which the woman can fulfill. Ibsen in *Little Eyolf* dealt with a far more dangerous type of exclusive passion, in which sex was a dominating and tragic factor.

The self-restriction imposed nevertheless had its moments of strain for Shaw, not the least in the intoxicated friendship with Mrs. Patrick Campbell which may have been intensified by it, and Shaw was not completely honest to Harris in this (he was, of course, warding him off dangerous ground as his biographer). But in essence he had found his haven; it suited him, and there was never any serious question of his leaving it once found.

An account, however brief, of his political life cannot be concluded without reference to his long service on the St. Pancras Borough Council—known in his time, 1897 to 1903, as the St. Pancras Vestry. He served on the Public Health, Parliamentary, Electricity, Housing and Drainage committees, thus gaining a varied and firsthand knowledge of local government in operation, much of which penetrated into his plays. In 1904 he stood as a Labour candidate for the London County Council, but failed to get elected.

As London Borough Councillor he wrote *The Commonsense of Municipal Trading,* still a classic of its kind in local government circles; shook the Victorian councillors by demanding logically but unprudishly that women should serve on the committee dealing with the building of public conveniences; took an active part in discussion of the administration of the Education Act, pleading for tolerance in education for the children's sakes, irrespective of whether "their parents be Established Churchmen, Free Churchmen, Roman Catholics or Jews"; and generally showed a thoroughly practical grasp of where true economy lay in the public interest ("A vigorous County Council, spending money freely on public health, convenience, and safety, saves the ratepayer more than it costs him," he wrote. "It is better to pay a shilling more to the rate collector than a couple of pounds more to the doctor.")

Whatever Shaw's enemies could say about him, it was never that he lacked public spirit, or spared himself in the interests of the community at large.

Chapter 3

"Corno di Bassetto"

A CATECHISM IN a journal once asked Bernard Shaw what was his first real success. His answer was succinct: "Never had any. Success, in that sense, is a thing that comes to you, and takes your breath away, as it came to Byron and Dickens and Kipling. What came to me was repeated failure. By the time I wore it down I knew too much to care about either failure or success."

This was strictly true: no genius had a more prolonged early struggle for recognition. Shaw came to London in 1876, and in 1885, the first year in which things might be said really to look up for him as a journalist, his total earnings reached the sum of £117 0s. 3d. The year was a turning point for him and it came, as journalistic opportunity always did and still does, not initially from personal ability but from a useful personal contact.

The contact was William Archer, the famous dramatic critic and (as a Scot with Norwegian family connections) first translator of the plays of Henrik Ibsen into English. His intellectual effect on Shaw was to be wide, for he instilled into Shaw his own passion for Ibsen which was to be an irrupting lava in Shaw's own dramatic criticism, and in his whole conception of the function of drama as a playwright. He was the first man to suggest to Shaw—who says he had never thought of it—that he should write a play. And he was to prove in himself perhaps the closest and warmest of all Shaw's friends, their lifelong regard unshaken by temperamental differences: the dour Scot looking askance at the Puckish exploits of the Irish buffoon, and as an admirer of the "well-made play" of Sardou and Pinero having grave doubts to the end about the validity of Shaw's claim to be a dramatist in this sense. All of which Shaw took in good part and without turning a hair in personal resentment, as was always his way.

Their meeting was characteristic. "In 1885 William Archer found me in the British Museum Reading Room, poring over Deville's French version of Karl Marx's *Capital,* with the orchestral score of Wagner's *Tristan und Isolde* beside it." No doubt intrigued by this dual and incongruous range of study—for he was not without his own quiet Scots sense of dry humor—Archer took the penniless young man (actually his senior by a few months) in hand: "with such success," wrote Shaw, "that the *Pall Mall Gazette,* then still extant, sent me books to review; and the appointment of art critic to *The World,* which Archer was for the moment doubling with his regular function of dramatic critic, was transferred to me."

This transference came about at Archer's own wish, for he had told the Editor, Edmund Yates, that he knew nothing about art, and only consented himself nominally to take the post if Shaw came along with him to the art shows. Yates had shocked the integrity of the Scot by saying, unperturbed, that ignorance of an art was the best qualification for criticizing it; and Shaw shocked him further by agreeing with Yates: "You will learn all you need to know by looking at pictures." This had, of course, been his own method of art education in Dublin and London, and was the basis of his considerable knowledge of music gained at home and in the concert hall: a method based on study of vocal and orchestral scores and listening to music in performance, which was the untrained Wagner's method. The bald statement is challengeable, of course, but not on the fundamental grounds on which Shaw, if not Yates, really based it. Too much technical "knowledgeability" can not only make criticism unreadable—as some musicologists have made it today—but it can distort judgment by imposing dogmas the genius will nearly always disregard, and distort the critic's own musical "ear" by substituting too much reading of music notation for careful listening. It is a reason why today some critics of high technical knowledge sometimes stagger one by their apparent inability to distinguish unsteady, insensitive or even off-pitch singers from great ones: a defect of musical "ear" of which Shaw, who heard and recognized the greatest singers of his time—and the great were not even then numerous—and separated them vigorously from the mediocre, would have been incapable.

Archer, full of conscientious scruples, pressed Shaw to accept the payments he received as official art critic, but Shaw returned his check with typical independence: "The idea of one man sucking another man's brains is a depraved individualistic idea. No man has a right of property in the ideas of which he is the mouthpiece . . . If I am to be paid for what I suggested to you, for example, the painters must be paid for what they suggested to me."

On the whole the last sentence is not a bad summing up of the indictment—often made by creative writers, actors and musicians—that criticism is a "bastard" profession and the critic a parasite in the world of art. Fortunately for his readers—who are, after all, the people most directly served by criticism and its true *raison d'être*—Shaw did not carry his integrity this far; and literature, drama and music are the richer (and certainly the livelier) for the years he spent earning his living as a critic.

His rejection of Archer's check precipitated Archer's resignation, persuading Yates to appoint Shaw officially his successor—his payment being 5d. a line. But art criticism, although his knowledge of it was considerable for that time, was not to be Shaw's function in life. The book reviewing on *The Pall Mall Gazette* had ceased because Shaw's integrity made it impossible for him to review a certain book until he had spent a year studying the subject—the review by that time of course being long overdue (later in life he was meticulous in delivering copy before the deadline; but by then, of course, he had all the subjects about which he wrote at his fingers' ends). The art criticism in *The World* ended equally abruptly in 1889, when a new woman owner suggested Shaw should write favorable reviews of pictures painted by her friends, and the outraged but far from speechless critic found his articles printed with interpolations of her own which he had never written.

He shook the dust of *The World* off his feet but returned to it as music critic a year later, in succession to Louis Engel, described by Shaw as "the best hated musical critic in Europe," who had got into some trouble which forced him to flee the country. But by then, under the frivolous name of Corno di Bassetto, which he was to use for all his music criticism, Shaw had already been functioning for over a year on the new London evening newspaper founded and edited by T. P. O'Connor, *The Star*. This made its first appearance on January 17, 1888. Shaw had been engaged on the second day of its existence as a leader writer at the suggestion of O'Connor's chief lieutenant, H. W. Massingham, later first editor of *The New Statesman and Nation*; but politically his progressive socialist leaders proved too hot for the liberal O'Connor to handle, and on Shaw's more or less requested resignation he was reinstated on the paper as music critic.

Critics at that time were expected to be anonymous—a fashion not at all welcome to Shaw. After toying with "the Count di Luna" from Verdi's *Il Trovatore,* he chose with *panache* for his new role the pseudonym "Corno di Bassetto," which was in fact the Italian name for the basset horn, an instrument last heard of in the time of Mozart and succeeded in orchestras by the bass clarinet. It was used by Mozart in his *Requiem* and had, according to Shaw, "a peculiar watery melancholy" and "a total absence of any richness or passion in its tone. If I had heard a note of it by 1888, I should not have selected its name for a character I intended to be sparkling."

Sparkling di Bassetto certainly was; its being an axiom of Shaw's that criticism should be amusing and highly readable with "a solid substratum of genuine criticism"—the substratum in this case being provided not only by his knowledge of music but of "political economy." Some of this last he hoped to get by the unsuspecting O'Connor, who had shifted him to the music column under the innocent delusion that there he would be completely harmless.

He was paid two guineas a week, which when he resigned from art criticism on *The World* became his only then source of income from journalism. But although his reputation through these articles increased his salary did not, and on February 28, 1890, he was forced to write to Massingham pointing out that the paper had owed him £7 0s. 1d. since March 30, 1889, for expenses, which did not include travel outside London for music festivals to places like Amsterdam and Bayreuth: expensive trips in the cause of his art which he seems—as the critic of integrity and enthusiasm still sometimes does today—to have taken voluntarily with no expectation of reimbursement beyond payment for the article.

He was therefore ready enough to leave *The Star* when offered the position of music critic on *The World* at five guineas a week, his first review—still as Corno di Bassetto—on the new paper appearing on May 28, 1890, and opening with a characteristic broadside of Wagnerian crusading fired at Covent Garden from a cannon of Irish hyperbole:

Something had better be done about this Royal Italian Opera. I have heard Gounod's *Faust* not less than ninety times within the last ten or fifteen years; and I have had enough of it. Here is *Tristan und Isolde,* which we can no longer afford to do without now that all the errand boys in New York can whistle it from end to end: yet to hear it I have to go to Germany. . . . *Tristan* is more than thirty years old; and as the composer died in 1883, at the age of seventy, I am sanguine as to the possibility of driving Mr. Harris to produce it presently as "Wagner's new opera."

His way of combining entertaining reporting with critical comment on the performance of the great followed later in the same article:

Brother Jean's[1] voice is better than it was last year. He sang *Salve dimora* very finely indeed; and when the audience, foolishly disappointed at his not taking the high C from his chest, hesitated a moment at the end, he gave them to understand, gracefully but firmly, that he had done his duty, and now expected them to do theirs. Whereupon, abashed, they gave him a salvo of prolonged and reverent applause. Brother Jean is still vaguely romantic rather than intelligent in his acting. The only part in *Faust* I ever saw him act reasonably was Valentine; but that, of course, was in his baritone days. D'Andrade falls very short of him in the part. In an opera company, D'Andrade passes for a good actor because he always makes it plain that he knows what the opera is about; but when this intellectual triumph becomes a little more common, he will find his place hard to hold. Would any really fine actor sing *Dio possente*—that tremblingly earnest prayer of a simple-minded young soldier—with the air of a man obstreperously confident that no difficulty could be made over any application from a baritone hall-marked with the unreticent throatiness familiar to patrons of the Paris Opéra?

In the reference to the interpretation of *Dio possente* we recognize how much Shaw's knowledge of the theatre and acting contributed to the value of his criticism of opera. For opera is acted with the expression and coloring

[1] The tenor Jean de Reszke, whose equally famous and popular baritone brother, Edouard, had disappointed the audience by failing to appear at this performance of *Faust* owing to illness. The French opera, as customary at 'the Royal Italian Opera' at Covent Garden at this time, was sung in Italian.

of the *voice,* as Shakespeare is, no less than with brain, face and body. One wonders what Shaw would have written of Hans Hotter, Ludwig Weber and Hermann Uhde, three superlative actor-singers of Wagner in our time, whose inflections of voice define every thought and emotion while they present the characters impressively or movingly in terms of stance, facial expression and gesture. Hotter as Wotan, a towering and anguished Olivier transported to Valhalla, with uplifted arms that seem to span the cosmos, a rage like fire, and a profound pathos and tenderness in farewell; Weber in the morose black evil of Hagen or the gentle, saintly irradiance of the aged Knight of the Grail, Gurnemanz, the deeply grooved lines of his face falling into a mask Satanic or tenderly spiritual; the younger, tall, gracefully slender Uhde, spitting menace as a Klingsor like a fallen Lucifer, contrasting the flawed nobilities of the darkly envious Telramund, the suffering Amfortas and the reluctant betrayer, Gunther, and presenting a Wotan (classical Olympus to Hotter's storm-tossed Valhalla) of noble purpose and fractured, bitter heart, with a *Das Ende* of mystic and enthralled tragic prevision—these are the types of actor-singer that both Wagner and Shaw were searching for, artists who if stripped of the music as a means of expression would remain outstanding and intelligent actors by any standards in any form of theatre.

It is a measure of Shaw's supremacy that few opera critics still have any genuine knowledge or appreciation of acting subtleties, or show signs of realizing that other singers at Covent Garden or the Metropolitan Opera have a certain dramatic lack in these parts, in comparison with these three supreme interpreters of them, and that the lack is serious to the operas. Shaw would have known the difference, as any actor or good dramatic critic does instantly. The combination of the physical gift of a fine voice with high musical and dramatic intelligence is rare but by a dispensation of Providence not unknown (Maria Callas, Tito Gobbi and Cesare Siepi, finest actor of Shaw's favorite, *Don Giovanni,* are other outstanding examples in our time), and as a critic Shaw had the ability to recognize, and analyze, both the musical and dramatic facets of a performance. His ear was as good as his brain and eye; but he was by no means only a "performance critic." Owing to his long study of music scores from adolescence, his knowledge of the works given, concert and operatic, was thoroughly sound, making possible that detailed analysis of individual points of performance without which criticism is unconstructive and indeed suspect, but also giving him standards of judgment which made him a prophet—and often a true prophet—of the music and composers of his time most likely to survive their contemporary assessment.

He worked on *The Star* from 1889 to 1890, and *The World* from 1890 to 1894, and when these articles on music were collected and published in four volumes, nearly forty years later, they were a revelation to many music critics. Few or none had till then realized the extent of Shaw's musical knowledge, for his work as a music critic had long been overshadowed by his greater fame as a dramatist, political essayist and indulged buffoon. There had been a general impression that because he wrote entertainingly and non-technically, for the general reader, he did not know what he was talking about. He fully realized this would happen, and heartily loathed musicological jargon.

His integrity was absolute even if disconcerting to the artist at the receiving end. Of a performance of the musical play *Dorothy*, then being acted on tour for the 788th time, he wrote: "Dorothy herself, a beauteous young lady of distinguished mien, with an immense variety of accents ranging from the finest Tunbridge Wells English (for genteel comedy) to the broadest Irish (for repartee and low comedy), sang without the slightest effort and without the slightest point, and was all the more desperately vapid because she suggested artistic gifts wasting in complacent abeyance": adding of the tenor singing opposite her, that he "was evidently counting the days until death should release him from the part of Wilder."

The point of this review of an obscure touring company cannot be fully understood unless it is known that the singer of the part of Dorothy was Shaw's sister Lucy, and the tenor her husband, Charles Butterfield!

Shaw had his fun with singers—like the tenor who, he declared, hit his top C with such enthusiasm that he fell right over it and a semitone down on the other side—and his criticism cannot always have endeared him to the young Paderewski: appreciation of his phenomenal execution, charm and "dash of humor" being mixed with a tart rapping over the knuckles for his "Richard III" barnstorming methods and violence in *fortissimo* ("He goes to the point at which a piano huddles itself up and lets itself be beaten instead of unfolding the richness and color of its tone"). The humor, which dazzles us—and it is difficult even now to read these seventy-year-old reviews without constantly laughing out loud—must have carried some sharp arrowheads into the hearts of its receivers. Yet the bubbling spirit of fun makes it very difficult to resent it as one resents the pseudohumorous, heavy-handed assaults of some critics, musical and dramatic, of later times; for Shaw always gives sound reasons for his judgments, his language is wittily apt, and one senses him absolutely devoid of spite. Moreover, on the question of music generally his eclectic taste and background (preserved in spite of his deliberate crusade for Wagner, then badly needed in England) give him a balance and understanding notable, and even freshly illuminating, even today.

"All my musical self-respect," he confesses, "is based on my keen appreciation of Mozart's work. It is still as true as it was before the Eroica symphony existed, that there is nothing better in art than Mozart's best. . . . We have had Beethoven, Schubert, Mendelssohn, Schumann, Götz and Brahms since his time: we have even had Dr. Parry, Prof. Stanford, Mr. Cowen, Dr. Mackenzie and Sir Arthur Sullivan; but the more they have left the Mozart quartet or quintet behind, the further it comes out ahead in its perfection of temper and refinement of consciousness. In ardent regions where all the rest are excited and vehement, Mozart alone is completely self-possessed: where they are clutching their bars with a grip of iron and forging them with Cyclopean blows, his gentleness of touch never deserts him: he is considerate, economical, practical under the same pressure of inspiration that throws your Titan into convulsions." And for Mozart he has no barbs, only an affectionate and fanciful acceptance, as when he writes of the *Requiem* that "in the few numbers—or parts of numbers—in that work which are pure Mozart, the corpse is left out. There is no shadow of death anywhere on Mozart's music. Even his own funeral was a failure. It was dispersed by a shower of rain; and to this day nobody knows where he was buried or whether he was buried at all or not. My own belief is that he was not. Depend on it, they had no sooner put up their umbrellas and bolted for the nearest shelter than he got up, shook off his bones into the common grave of the people, and soared off into universality."

All this was written when Mozart was under a cloud in general critical opinion. And when Parry, Stanford, Sullivan and their fellows were accepted by most English music critics as serious composers beyond reproach. He was ahead of his time, too, in writing of Beethoven's Ninth Symphony that he would rather have it, "even from the purely musical point of view, than all the other eight put together, and to whom, besides, it is religious music, and its performance a celebration rather than an entertainment. I am highly susceptible to the force of all religious music, no matter to what Church it belongs; but the music of my own Church—for which I may be allowed, like other people, to have a partiality—is to be found in the *Die Zauberflöte* and the Ninth Symphony."

It is a revealing confession of a side often lost in the clown: the aesthete of deep and even spiritual purpose. And with his knowledge of the technical processes he had —again rare in his time—a clear vision of the historical "placing" of great music, its relevance and perpetuity in time. He saw, as Professor Edward J. Dent remarked in his article on Corno di Bassetto in *G.B.S. 90,* that "Mozart was the consummation of an epoch, and that after his death it was impossible to go on imitating him. A new departure had to be made altogether, and it was Cherubini who initiated it, followed by Beethoven, Weber and the Romantics. And he saw clearly in 1891 that Wagner too was the end of a period and not a beginning."

What Shaw actually wrote in *The Perfect Wagnerite* was:

> The success of Wagner has been so prodigious that to his dazzled disciples it seems that the age of what he called 'absolute' music must be at an end, and the musical future destined to be an exclusively Wagnerian one inaugurated at Bayreuth. All great geniuses produce this illusion. Wagner did not begin a movement: he consummated it. He was the summit of the nineteenth-century school of dramatic music in the same sense as Mozart was the summit (the word is Gounod's) of the eighteenth-century school. And those who attempt to carry on his Bayreuth tradition will assuredly share the fate of the forgotten purveyors of second hand Mozart a hundred years ago.

The ignorance and denigration of Carl Orff—the Orff of the *Antigonae* and *Oedipus Tyrannus*—by many critics today equals that of Wagner in Shaw's time. But he too, seeming to stand alone, may prove to be a summit of music drama in this century as Wagner was in the last, stripping music to its inmost muscle and bone (in spite of his enormous and mainly percussive orchestra) and fashioning it absolutely to the rhythmic complexities and emotions of Sophoclean tragedy, so that the drama becomes intensified in a new way, without the post-Wagnerian excesses of Richard Strauss and his librettist von Hoffmanstahl. But as in the case of Wagner's *Tristan und Isolde,* it may well be English audiences will have to wait thirty years, until after the composer's death, to see Orff's *Antigonae* or *Oedipus* and judge for themselves.

Shaw's experience with Lee helped him to appreciate that the vocal requirements in the way of mellifluousness, line and style for singing Wagner differed not at all from those for other operas: "Wagner meant his music to be sung with the most exquisite sensitiveness in point of quality of tone and precision of pitch, exactly as Mozart did." And he was no less alive to similar needs in the orchestral playing, castigating the coarseness of the orchestra in performances of *The Ring* by a German company under Gustav Mahler in 1892: comparing the brass to "a huge tribe of mongrels, differing chiefly in size. I felt that some ancestor of the trombones had been guilty of a mésalliance with a bombardon; that each cornet, though itself already an admittedly half-bred trumpet, was further disgracing itself by a leaning towards the flügel horn; and that the mother of the horns must have run away with a whole military band." He adds, with a vividness painfully recognizable to the practiced *Ring*-goer, that the Rhine sounded like "a river of treacle, and rather lumpy treacle at that." Yet Shaw never lost his balance as to the effect of the whole work. "The impression created by the performance was extraordinary, the gallery cheering wildly at the end of each act. Everybody was delighted with the change from the tailor-made operatic tenor in velvet and tights to the wild young hero who forges his own weapons and tans his own coat and buskins. We all breathed that vast orchestral atmosphere of fire, air, earth and water with unbounded relief and invigoration."

He beats a drum not only for Wagner but for every necessary operatic reform from matters of staging, performance and the compulsory slimming of singers, to the extension of rehearsal time: marking out for special comment Sir Charles Santley's story in his *Reminiscences* of his first appearance as Don Giovanni: "As usual, I had one rehearsal the morning of the day of performance. Mario, who was always a late riser, did not come in until we were half-way through the rehearsal." In this he was not merely ahead of the opera houses of his day but sometimes of our own, as more than one conscientious contemporary international singer can ruefully testify.

Shaw as a critic was meticulous in attending recitals by unknown or lesser-known performers as well as the established artists: to them his criticism was often helpful and his prophecies and dismissals were not often at fault. And of composers, too, his deep knowledge of the classical made him a good judge: he was not easily moved by current assessments, especially overoptimistic assessments, knowing that the lasting reputation is rare in any generation. He later realized the preëminence of Elgar, and greatly admired Vaughan Williams, without ever having joined his colleagues in putting Stanford, Parry and their like on pinnacles of future fame.

He raged about the addiction of music festivals and composers to oratorio, at the expense of instrumental music; agitated for municipal orchestras; and bitterly denounced Cosima Wagner's intention of reserving the right of performing *Parsifal* to Bayreuth exclusively: "In other words, the whole world is to be robbed of one of its most precious heirlooms for the glorification of a stupid little Bavarian town about as large as Notting Hill Gate and its neighborhood." He had elsewhere drawn an unidealized picture of the commercial tourism atmosphere round the Bayreuth Festspielhaus, and was no tolerator of any religious sham attached to the performance of *Parsifal* there.

And within a few years of Wagner's death in 1883, he was already writing with profound prophetic insight of the need to throw off the "Bayreuth tradition" and keep Wagner's operas ever fresh along the newest lines of theatrical staging: a revolution not achieved until half a century later, when Wagner's grandsons, Wieland and Wolfgang, have achieved the complete imaginative severance from the past anticipated and advocated by Shaw.

In all these things, in fact, he was clearing a path since followed: though still incompletely where municipal orchestras are concerned.

In 1898 he crystallized all he had learned, analyzed and philosophically understood from *The Ring* in a small book or long essay, *The Perfect Wagnerite*, which to anyone who has really studied this cycle of music dramas in text and performances remains the most remarkable exposition yet made of them, because unlike most critical essays it is the work of one creative genius on another, which means one able to put into revealing language the implications behind the technical structure and the processes of art generally, in addition to giving the type of story and music analysis which can be found in other works on the subject. His understanding of the dramatic symbolism and philosophy of the works was certainly well ahead of his time.

Naturally he had a close sympathy with Wagner as sociologist and musician. People ignorant of Wagner tend to assume that Shaw was merely reading into *The Ring* his own political views and twisting Wagner's allegory to do so. St. John Ervine takes this view, and as the author of a book on Wagner's operas I can state categorically it is nonsense. Wagner knew very much what he was doing in this respect and Shaw, who had read his letters to his friend, the revolutionist Roeckel, as well as closely studied the operas themselves, knew that he knew. This does not mean he was uncritical; indeed on certain points, most of all the more operatic construction of *Die Götterdämmerung* and the treatment of the Brünnhilde-Siegfried immolation-for-love themes—which he compares with Shelley's panacea of love as a redemption of the world's ills—he was by his nature out of sympathy. Nevertheless, what he has to say on the subject is always worth reading and often sound as criticism, and at times he throws a fine illumination not only on Wagner but on Wagner's influences on his own plays later. He is notable and fairly rare, too, in fully appreciating *Das Rheingold,* the Prologue to *The Ring* tetralogy, which is frequently underrated: seeing in it "the whole tragedy of human history and the whole horror of the dilemmas from which the world is shrinking today." This was as true in 1962 as in 1898, for the world does not easily learn from its mistakes.

Being an artist himself, he never falls into the mediocre critic's trap of trying meticulously to fit a creative writer into one harmonious pattern: "do not forget that an allegory is never quite consistent except when it is written by someone without dramatic faculty, in which case it is unreadable." Wagner's personality he described as "manifold," explaining commonsensically the extreme philosophical cleavage between *Siegfried,* an embodiment of human optimism and the Will to Live, and *Tristan und Isolde,* its theme and music saturated with sorrow and the Schopenhauer death-wish.

"Wagner was not a Schopenhauerite every day in the week, nor even a Wagnerite. His mind changes as often as his mood"; he "can be quoted against himself almost without limit, much as Beethoven's adagios could be quoted against his scherzos if a dispute arose between two fools as to whether he was a melancholy man or a merry one." "The truth is, we are apt to deify men of genius, exactly as we deify the creative force of the universe, by attributing to logical design what is the result of blind instinct. What Wagner meant by 'true Art' is the operation of the artist's instinct, which is just as blind as any other instinct. Mozart, asked for an explanation of his works, said frankly 'How do I know?' Wagner, being a philosopher and critic as well as a composer, was always looking for moral explanations of what he had created; and he hit on several very striking ones, all different."

Shaw, being above all things practical, is fully aware too of how much the span of years over which Wagner created *The Ring* inevitably affected it by the time he had completed *Götterdämmerung*. "No man whose mind is alive and active as Wagner's was to the day of his death, can keep his political and spiritual opinions, much less his philosophic consciousness, at a standstill for a quarter of a century until he finishes an orchestral score."

This means that while acute enough in noting occasional philosophical or even dramatic irrelevances, he retains a very just estimate of the greatness and symbolic power of the whole work, bound together by the figure of Wotan which he recognizes as, more than Siegfried, the true tragic motivating force of drama and allegory.

"Wotan was the half-way house, as it were, between god and man—the whole point of *The Ring* being the acceptance of Man as the highest possible expression of life.

"In the old-fashioned orders of creation the supernatural personages are invariably conceived as greater than man, for good or evil. In the modern humanitarian order as adopted by Wagner, Man is the highest . . . the world is waiting for Man to redeem it from the lame and cramped government of the gods. . . .

"Godhead means to Wagner infirmity and compromise, and manhood strength and integrity. . . . The God, since his desire is toward a higher and fuller life, must long in his inmost soul for the advent of that greater power whose first work, though this he does not see as yet, must be his own undoing."

But Wotan, for this very reason of his farseeing wisdom

and too-human error, is a sympathetic creation very unlike Shelley's totally evil Jupiter: "Wagner, an older, more experienced man than the Shelley of 1819, understood Wotan and pardoned him, separating him tenderly from all the compromising alliances to which Shelley fiercely held him, making the truth and heroism which overthrow him the children of his inmost heart; and representing him as finally acquiescing in and working for his own supersession and annihilation."

"The children of his inmost heart": one could not more finely describe the creation of Brünnhilde and Siegmund, born of Wotan for the destruction of the outworn laws of the gods that bind him and the world, and of Siegfried, Siegmund's son: throbbing echoes of his own conscience whose disobedience outrages him because he recognizes it as stemming from his own inmost desire, so that he loves them for it even though it hurtles him from power.

It is illuminating that Shaw recognized and accepted this humanity in Wotan, for the merging of the symbol with the human being is something Wagner derives from Shakespeare. Shaw felt himself instinctively bound to resent Shakespeare, for his own dramatic springs were intellectual not emotional, and to achieve production of his own plays he needed managements like the Lyceum to be released from the stranglehold of Shakespeare. But with Wagner he could appreciate, if not always concur, partly through his musical "ear." "To enjoy *Tristan* it is only necessary to have had one serious love affair; and though the number of persons possessing this qualification is popularly exaggerated, yet there are enough to keep the work alive and vigorous . . . the truth is that all the merely romantic love scenes ever penned are pallid beside the second act of *Tristan*." And although he was out of sympathy with the panacea of love in the closing scene of *Götterdämmerung*, as with the death-wish of *Tristan*, he could still accept *The Ring* through its music and its allegorical key.

"The only faith which any reasonable disciple can gain from *The Ring* is not in love, but in life itself as a tireless power which is continually driving onward and upward."

The derivations from this in *Man and Superman* are obvious. In fact Shaw's writing on Wagner is still important not only in itself but in its revelation of the very close affinity of idea between the two at times in creation. Undoubtedly Shaw was influenced as a dramatist by his study of Wagner, though he expanded and molded the influences according to his own different temperament and colder intellectualism. The ideas of Superman and Life Force (not of course limited to Wagner but deriving from Schopenhauer and Nietzsche) were transmuted rather than borrowed by him, although he has an illuminating passage in his book on the price which Wotan must pay for his Olympian power, symbolized in the building of Valhalla: "As a god, he is to be great, secure, and mighty; but he is also to be passionless, affectionless, wholly impartial"; a price Wotan in the event is unable to pay, thus precipitating his own downfall.

Shaw's supermen—Caesar, for instance—have not the same weaknesses, though sharing Siegfried's indifference to fear. Caesar's "He who has never hoped can never despair" is the mature twist to Siegfried's youthful hopefulness, as is Juan's "It is not death that matters, but the fear of death." But Shaw was sharp enough and human enough in *Man and Superman* to give the Devil opposing the idea his strongest argument: "Beware the pursuit of the Superman: it leads to an indiscriminate contempt for the Human." And he was aware of the cost, that loneliness which assails the great: "I have found flocks and pastures, men and cities, but no other Caesar," says his Caesar; and the loneliness of the saint is overcome in his Joan of Arc's great cry: "What is my loneliness, compared with the loneliness of God?" Wotan, too, is a lonely God; hence the tragedy of the rift for him with Brünnhilde, the daughter who is his only close friend and understands, because she is an expression of, his own will and conscience.

In other respects Shaw and Wagner share the dramatic conception of the "wise Ancient." Gurnemanz in *Parsifal* and Wotan: Captain Shotover and the Ancients in *Back to Methuselah:* the link is fairly obvious. So, too, is that between Beckmesser in *Die Meistersinger* and de Stogumber in *Saint Joan*—both a satirical tilt at the conventional mind. The destruction of man suggested in Lilith was only, for Shaw, the beginning of a new experiment in life—Wagner's occasional despair he never touched on. But life—human and intellectual—was his theme, and, a prose writer and not a poet, he had nothing of Wagner's obsession with the elemental forces of Nature, although he appreciated the artistic form they took in Wagner's music. His production demands were limited (basically a room and chairs for discussion) whereas Wagner demanded that his ranging cosmic imagination should be given literal stage shape and form. Yet strangely the affinities coalesce; and *The Perfect Wagnerite* remains as a living tribute from artist to artist, from the ascetic to the aesthete, united in the creative instinct and the questing processes of the intellect.

No study of Shaw's musical side is irrelevant to himself or his work. It was an education, he himself wrote, that never ceased, having "gone on from Rossini, Meyerbeer and Verdi to Wagner, from Beethoven to Sibelius, from British dilutions of Handel and Mendelssohn to the genuine English music of Elgar and Vaughan Williams and from the wholetone mode of Debussy and the chromatic mode of Schönberg to the experiments of Cyril Scott in the technical chaos which ensued when the forbidden consecutives and unprepared unresolved discords and 'false relations' of the old textbooks became the latest fashion.

Much of it has proved the soundness of Oscar Wilde's precept 'Avoid the latest fashion or you will be hopelessly out of date in six months.' "

More than his theatre criticism (limited by the fewer lasting works then being performed, outside Shakespeare and Ibsen), it reveals his range of expression and catholicity of taste. He had no violent prejudices, being still able to capture with pleasure some of the flavor of Donizetti and Bellini even when enmeshed in the Book of Revelation that was Wagner; and this is reflected in his plays where—it has sometimes been said against him—there are no real villains and therefore no real dramatic, as opposed to intellectual, conflicts.

Music was "so important in my development," he wrote to St. John Ervine in old age, "that nobody can really understand my art without being soaked in symphonies and operas, in Mozart, Verdi and Meyerbeer, to say nothing of Handel, Beethoven and Wagner, far more completely than in the literary drama and its poets and playwrights."

"Harley Granville-Barker was not far out," he noted elsewhere, "when, at a rehearsal of one of my plays, he cried out 'Ladies and Gentlemen: will you please remember that this is Italian opera.' "

Shaw's weekly page on music continued in *The World* for four years until 1894, when its editor, Edmund Yates, for whom he had a great admiration and who allowed him a free hand, died. Shaw, feeling he must find another editor with Yates' qualities, immediately resigned; but yielded to the new editor's plea that he should continue until the end of the season, in case his resignation were taken to reflect on him as editor.

His last two articles, on August 1 and 8, were devoted to his visit to that year's Bayreuth Festival which had just taken place: thus aptly enough ending on a Wagnerian note and recording for history the first Bayreuth production of *Lohengrin*—eighteen years after Wagner opened the theatre! His lively criticism of the standard of German singing —or, as he bluntly calls it, "shouting"—in *Parsifal* and *Tannhäuser* also suggests that Wagner's own insistence on the necessity for beauty of tone and line in the singing of his operas was something already ignored in his own theatre eleven years after his death. Significantly, Hermann Levi, the conductor, who had known and worked with Wagner on the first production of *Parsifal,* could not begin to understand Shaw's criticism, made with typical lack of inhibition when they briefly met.

Shaw was enlightened in noting that the non-German singers of *Lohengrin,* who included Nordica and Van Dyck, excelled the German in true Wagnerian singing style, and his criticism remains pungent today, when some of the best singers of Wagner in living memory, at Bayreuth and elsewherc, have been not Germans but Scandinavians like Kirsten Flagstad and Birgit Nilsson, the greatest Brünnhildes of the immediate past and of today. We still know the kind of singers meant by Shaw when he commented on the apparent strangeness to Germans of the notion that "it is more truly virile to sing like a man than a bullock"; though they are not only German and unfortunately still encouraged by opera managements and critics who lack Shaw's sensitivity, in Germany itself and elsewhere.

Shaw's strictures on orchestral and instrumental roughness were also sharp, and it is probable standards in this case were much below those of today, when competition is much greater both among executants and international orchestras, and the difficulties of some modern scores make higher demands on the players.

To the last, as music critic as in his other capacities throughout life, he kept his independence of judgment, refused to bow to legendary humbug, and was fearless in the lion's jaws not only in stating an opinion, but giving valid technical reasons for it.

He never returned to regular music criticism: pointing out however that this was only because the overlapping of concert, opera and dramatic events in London made the two professions impracticable. But he strongly insisted there is a critical loss on both sides when the critic of the one art is ignorant of the other, and instanced Lewes ("the most able and brilliant critic between Hazlitt and our own contemporaries"), Archer and Walkley of *The Times,* all knowledgeable on drama and music, in support of his case. The limitations of specialization are even more marked today, and reinforce Shaw's view.

Chapter 4

The Critic and the Theatre

IN SEPTEMBER, 1894, *The Saturday Review* was bought by the picturesque journalist-adventurer Frank Harris: "the very man for me," wrote Shaw, who was not to be bowled over by a wild reputation—the very antithesis of his own—when in addition the man, as he was convinced Harris did, "knew good writing from bad; and preferred good to bad." When Harris offered him the post of dramatic critic on *The Saturday Review,* at £6 per week ("not bad in those days," commented Shaw), he therefore accepted with alacrity. His first article appeared on January 5, 1895, and his last on May 21, 1898; by which time his increasing devotion to playwriting and the foot injury that led to his marriage made his relinquishment of his weekly London labor more or less inevitable.

"The drama being a much less segregated cult than music, my fame at once increased with a rush," he wrote in *Sixteen Self Sketches;* "and thenceforth for years my name seldom appeared in print without the adjective brilliant, which I disliked, as it suggested a glittering superficiality which I abhorred."

In fact, his work received some epithets very much the opposite of brilliant, especially in theatrical quarters. He was, he fails to add, the terror of the managements, including Sir Henry Irving's at the Lyceum, for he spared his flail nowhere where he felt there were tares to be destroyed. It was not a time of the slightest dramatic distinction in the English theatre, the mild "tea cup and saucer" revolution in the drama achieved by Tom Robertson in the 1860's having drifted into the only slightly less mild revolutionary "high society" dramas of Sir Arthur Pinero in the nineties. "A very little epoch, and a very little play," wrote Shaw of a revival of Robertson's "epoch-making" *Caste* after thirty years in 1897; but he well knew its significance in its own time was not by any means despicable. "The Robertsonian movement caught me as a boy; the Ibsen movement caught me as a man; and the next one will catch me as a fossil" was his characteristic comment.

His passion for Ibsen, to whose works Archer had introduced him, was of course the root cause of his dissatisfaction with the plays presented in the London theatre (and those produced by visiting foreign companies were mainly of the same level). But his mind had been developed on literature too—George Eliot, George Moore (to whose novels Archer had also introduced him) and Tolstoy, among others—and he was not the man to accept the rubbish then generally performed as the sole material for the theatre. One of the reasons for this low level of creative writing was the public taste for acting, the chief bait that drew it to the theatre. And it was his special fury that the actors had not learned to match their superlative gifts of visual and aural interpretation with a mental education which would have insisted on exercising them in plays which had some literary and intellectual merits: using, in fact, their minds as well as their too-facile emotions.

Hence his onslaught on the Lyceum, a museum atrophied in heavily cut versions of Shakespeare and out-of-date romantic melodramas fashioned to the unmistakable, but intensely personal, gifts of its principal actor, Irving; and to some degree his attack on Shakespeare himself as the god of the idolatry of an ignorant public which cared nothing for the fact (if, indeed, it realized it) that it was seeing only mutilated versions of his plays, and still less for the kind of drama that was intellectually about to revolutionize the theatre. This meant, of course, not only the plays of Ibsen but the plays of one George Bernard Shaw, whose wit had not yet pierced the public consciousness and sent audiences out of the theatre rocking with laughter—as it did later: too delighted and amused to object to the fact that they had been educated as well as entertained.

The fact is that Shaw, if not as eclectic in taste in drama as in music (which was inevitable, as he himself was a composer in the one and not in the other), had a genuine breadth of knowledge of his subject and this showed in his adverse criticisms no less than in his praise. If he did not always refrain from tearing the wings of butterflies, he did so—unlike some young tearers today—with a quick appreciation of a flash of color if it was there to note. His review of a dramatization of Marie Corelli's *The Sorrows of Satan* at the Shaftesbury Theatre in 1897 shows he was not too much a snob as not to know at first hand a great deal of the work of one of the most popular novelists of the day; and though his review could hardly have given Miss Corelli pleasure on the grounds of his assessment of her mental endowments, she could not have complained that its author had not properly studied her works or failed to appreciate her powers of imagination and sincere purpose.

When I say that Miss Corelli is sincere, I of course do not mean that she has ever acted on the assumption that her "religion" is real. But when she takes up her pen she imagines it to be real, because she has a prodigiously copious and fluent imagination, without, as far as I have been able to ascertain, the knowledge, the training, the observation, the critical faculty, the humor, or any other of the requirements and qualities which compel ordinary people to distinguish in some measure (and in some measure only; for the best of us is not wholly un-Corellian) between what they may sanely believe and what they would like to believe. Great works in fiction are the arduous victories of great minds over great imaginations: Miss Corelli's works are the cheap victories of a profuse imagination over an apparently commonplace and carelessly cultivated mind.

"Great works in fiction are the arduous victories of great minds over great imaginations." This is the kind of statement—a generalization, yet a blinding flash of truth—that marks Shaw over and over again as a great critic: meaning a critic whose values are scaled to understand greatness and recognize it in others.[1] But the earlier careful parenthesis—". . . in some measure only: for the best of us is not wholly un-Corellian"—is also characteristic, in that it shows him, contrary to uninformed popular belief, as a critic with the necessary springs of humility and self-understanding, devoid in his judgments of personal arrogance. Few critics of intellectual pretensions would dare to admit themselves "not wholly un-Corellian"; but Shaw was observant of human nature, not excluding his own, and he knew that the wholly un-Corellian, unimaginative artist, creative or critical, is worthless, a tinder too damp to ignite when struck.

He was characteristic, too, in deploring Miss Corelli's Satan for lacking the conviction of his villainy: "when it comes to the devil, I claim, like Brand, 'all or nothing.' A snivelling, remorseful devil, with his heart in the right place, sneaking about the area railings of heaven in the hope that he will presently be let in and forgiven, is an abomination to me." And his musical knowledge enabled him to see from how much operatic snooping Miss Corelli had derived some of her ideas, including *The Flying Dutchman* apotheosis at the end of *The Sorrows of Satan* and (which few even today would be informed enough to notice) the adaptation of the *Todesverkündigung* scene from *Die Walküre* in *Thelma.*

[1] Shortly before I wrote this a prominent young dramatic critic—a notorious butterfly-destroyer—referred to three plays by an equally young and promising playwright, Arnold Wesker, as a "mighty trilogy." The epithet might have been used by Shaw of the *Oresteia, Der Ring des Nibelungen* and *War and Peace*, and probably only after hesitation of *King Lear* and George Eliot's *Middlemarch*. This is what I mean by "values" in a critic.

The sociologist in him quickened his sensitivity to certain blunders of characterization which grew out of the stereotyped, wholly "theatrical" plays of the time:

> Réjane has brought us M. Maurice Donnay's *La Douloureuse,* in which a circle of disreputable people are represented as gaily sitting down to a champagne supper whilst the host lies suicided. Such false sociology is unpardonable. I can assure M. Donnay that disreputable people, having no nerve and no character, are always full of "heart." If their host committed suicide, they would burst into tears, see his ghost, commiserate his wife and children, and drink brandy very apologetically on the plea of being quite upset. And they would send all the flowers they could beg or buy on credit to heap on the coffin.

This is socially true, in a way few dramatists except Ibsen would have dared admit on the stage at the time; and Shaw's perspicacity is at possible fault (and it is a key to some of his own defects of character-drawing in his plays) only in failing to point out that a lot of this "heart" would be quite genuine to the owner of it, sentimentality and even true pity not being prerogatives of the reputable.

The same sociological sense set him raging at the use of small infants in shows which at that time went on until past 11 o'clock or midnight. A child's enjoyment of occasional amateur "theatricals" was one thing; but nightly work for a run of months "in a sort of delirium induced by the conflict between intense excitement and intense sleepiness" was quite another. Surprisingly few critics shared Shaw's view at the time or, even if fathers, as he was not, saw the difference clearly. "Truly, as Talleyrand said," commented the exasperated bachelor, "the father of a family is capable of anything."

His objection, nevertheless, had practical effect later in the laws governing the stage employment of children in England. His pen already wielded great strength, and theatre managements began to make reforms. Like Wagner, and for the same reasons, he was reformative in respect of stage production, and in this he knew what he was talking about. Wagner, the stepson of an actor who had also been a professional painter, had by training and background developed an "eye" as well as an "ear," unusual in many musicians. Shaw's earliest tutor, as we have seen, had been the National Gallery of Ireland, and he had functioned successfully as an art critic. Both men were looking for a new kind of theatre, for a new kind of music-drama and a new kind of drama; and Shaw well knew that Ibsen had had to turn from poetic dramas such as *Brand* because the stages of the time could only cope with short plays and strict realism, while Wagner, with some revolutionary lighting ideas shared by Adolph Appia, had had to build a new opera house at Bayreuth, on new architectural principles (including an orchestra out of sight under the stage, where it could not drown the singers but only balance instruments and voice), before his own music-dramas could be adequately staged. Shaw's criticisms of Bayreuth musically (after Wagner's death) had been stringent; but of the superb quality of the staging and dramatic production, compared with that in other European theatres of the period, he was never in doubt.

Of all this the average dramatic critic of his time was as blissfully ignorant as indeed dramatic critics and producers remained in this country until only a few years ago, when the experimental dramas of writers like Ionesco began to burst the seams of the proscenium stage and split it asunder for ever. (It is still doubtful if many of them strictly concerned with plays know anything of the most profoundly artistic and revolutionary stagings of all since 1951, those in the field of opera by Wieland Wagner, an artist whose imaginative symbolism is unique today in world theatres, though influenced in some measure by Gordon Craig, now over ninety years old.)

Producers, especially of Shakespeare, who had never written for a proscenium stage, had of course begun to experiment in their limited conditions much earlier, and in railing against Irving's mutilations of Shakespeare (to allow long tedious intervals while his heavy scenery was erected and dismantled) Shaw was merely anticipating them. In fact he was the first to welcome William Poel's reforms for the Elizabethan Stage Society, his review of Poel's *The Tempest* at the Mansion House in 1897 getting incisively to the heart of the matter of stage illusion:

> Mr. Poel says frankly, "See that singers' gallery up there! Well, let's pretend that it's the ship." We agree; and the thing is done. . . . The singing gallery makes no attempt to impose on us: it disarms criticism by unaffected submission to the facts of the case, and throws itself honestly on our fancy, with instant success. In the same way a rag doll is fondly nursed by a child who can only stare at a waxen simulacrum of infancy. A superstitious person left to himself will see a ghost in every ray of moonlight on the wall, and every old coat hanging on a rail; but make up a really careful, elaborate, plausible, picturesque, bloodcurdling ghost for him, and his cunning grin will proclaim that he sees through it at a glance. The reason is, not that a man can *always* imagine things more vividly than art can present them to him, but that it takes an altogether extraordinary degree of art to compete with the pictures which the imagination makes when it is stimulated by such potent forces as the maternal instinct, superstitious awe, or the poetry of Shakespeare.

But Shaw was balanced and no fanatic, in this as in all things: "There is no general rule, not even for any particular author. You can do best without scenery in *The Tempest* and *A Midsummer Night's Dream,* because the best scenery you can get will only destroy the illusion created by the poetry; but it does not at all follow that scenery will not improve a representation of *Othello.*" And his eye, trained on the world's greatest paintings, never allowed him to underestimate the quality of Irving's Lyceum productions from the purely *visual* point of view. He saw they were (whatever they did to the author) pictures composed by a master, in which both Irving and Ellen Terry took a creative part with their superbly dramatic and pictorial sense of plastic pose or movement.

Nevertheless, his highly practical feeling for production, later brought to bear on rehearsals of his own plays, is evident in his criticism, and critics who are the despair of theatre artists by their obvious confusion of "design" with "production" could profit from a study of Shaw's reviews. On acting he remains vivid and readable, with the same basis of knowledge founded on both common sense and stage sense. His insight into the all-over composition of a performance—the "wholeness" of characterization aimed at by the best actors—is rare outside the stage profession itself.

"With the greatest artists," he wrote in an article on Duse in June, 1895, "there soon commences an integrating of the points into a continuous whole, at which stage the actress appears to make no points at all, and to proceed in the most unstudied and 'natural' way. This rare consummation Duse has reached." He was unimpressed by the so-called "versatility" of "stock" acting; "stock companies" of Shaw's early days being formed on the basis of a large weekly repertoire of different plays, type-cast, as he pointed out, by a set of actors who turned out roughly the same performance—juvenile, "character" or romantic, according to their particular "line"—in every play.

To this mechanical representation of "character," based on the greasepaint box and a well-worn set of tricks, Shaw thought even the long-run system preferable: "the modern actor may at all events exhaust the possibilities of his part before it exhausts him" (he well knew, however, no star actor of quality could sustain a great part six nights a week all the year round, and maintain the highest standard at every performance).

His panacea was the kind of National Theatre many of

us would still welcome—and are still fighting for—in England today: "What we want in order to get the best work is a repertory theatre with alternative casts. If, for instance, we could have *Hamlet* running at the Lyceum with Sir Henry Irving and Miss Ellen Terry on Thursdays and Saturdays, Mr. Forbes-Robertson and Mrs. Patrick Campbell on Wednesdays and Fridays, and the other two days devoted to comedies in which all four could occasionally appear, with such comedians as Mr. Charles Wyndham, Mr. Weedon Grossmith, Mr. Bourchier, Mr. Cyril Maude, and Mr. Hawtrey, then we should have a theatre which we could invite serious people to attend without positively insulting them."

Sixty years after Shaw wrote, the Shakespeare Memorial Theatre at Stratford-on-Avon and the Aldwych Theatre in London, and the Old Vic in London and on tour, perform a repertoire on something like these principles; but the difference is there are no changes of cast (except those caused by indispositions) within one season and the greatest actors England can provide do not appear there except in isolated flashes. Shaw's vision was of a true National Theatre, in which in our own time Sir John Gielgud and Dame Peggy Ashcroft would alternate in the great tragedies and dramas with, say, Sir Laurence Olivier and Dame Edith Evans, Sir Donald Wolfit and Dame Sybil Thorndike, Sir Michael Redgrave and Dame Flora Robson; and in comedy would join a team headed by such masters of their line as Sir Alec Guinness, John Clements and Kay Hammond, Athene Seyler, Rex Harrison and Ian Carmichael (a brilliant, intelligent and stylish comedian whose invention under our modern commercial system has never been allowed to range into classic comedy).

It is a vision the audacity and splendor of which we can still acknowledge, and for the fruition of which, although the creation of a National Theatre has now been officially agreed, we still wait. But until it is realized the superb acting resources of the British theatre will never be properly combined and used; the best plays of the world given adequate presentation here; and our theatre take the supreme place it could in the European scene. The omission and need apply even more to the United States, where the indigenous dramas of a Tennessee Williams and Arthur Miller have no permanent home and comparison alongside world classics, and no tradition of team acting to support them.[2]

Shaw's crusading zeal for Ibsen makes it not surprising that he had a keen eye for the chraracterization of any actor in Ibsen's plays. Of Laurence Irving's Hjalmor Ekdal in *The Wild Duck* he gave a sharply balanced view, recognizing the one flaw and incidentally the real nature of interpretation needed: "His appearance proclaimed his weakness at once: the conceited ass was recognizable at a glance. This was not right; Hjalmar should impose on us at first." But it is more surprising to find that although (as a tub-thumping herald of Ibsen and the new drama) he did not spare Shakespeare the dramatist for his supposed faults—including (and Shaw was astonishingly off the mark here) faults of humanity and characterization—his understanding of acting did not fail him in his criticisms of many Shakespearean performances.

He is generally believed to have been a denigrator of Irving the actor; but although his own platonic but by no means unromantic relationship with Ellen Terry pricked him to unfairness towards Irving the man and manager,

[2] The opening of a repertory theatre under the direction of Mr. Elia Kazan in the new Lincoln Center for the Performing Arts in New York will help to redress this, although the company is at present intended to be a permanent one in which leading members of the profession will not necessarily appear. Sir Tyrone Guthrie's vision and experiment in the new theatre at Minneapolis may also have a wide influence. But Shaw's bolder plan of a National Theatre open to the greatest has still to be tried.

who (though Shaw never openly admitted this) held Ellen's heart and loyalty as well as keeping her from parts Shaw felt she ought to play, his criticism of Irving's acting is not severe by the strictest standards of impartiality. He always played, not Shakespeare's character, but Shakespeare's character transformed by the untransmutable personality and mannerisms of Sir Henry Irving, he wrote; but it was a fairly general criticism of Irving, most magnetic of actors, and has been made in varying degrees of most of the greatest actors of history. Irving was "multi-radiant," wrote Max Beerbohm in a classic study of the actor on his death; and he meant by this very much the same thing as Shaw did.

Of Irving's most outstanding personal quality—and it is a rare quality on the stage—which was his "distinction," Shaw was fully aware and admiring. His long association with his mother and Vandaleur Lee enabled him to understand not only the natural and acknowledged defects of Irving's voice, but also the voice production method—mainly nasal—he had developed and used to overcome them, and to give his voice resonance. His appreciation of some of his best performances—such as Iachimo—was generous as well as acute. And when on October 14, 1905, Irving died, and Shaw was asked by the *Neue Freie Presse* of Vienna to contribute an obituary notice, followed by an article on Ellen Terry, he summed up the preëminence of the Lyceum as it rested in these two: "Her incomparable beauty and his incomparable distinction: there lay the Lyceum magic." He realized, too, characteristically and memorably, how much the magic was pictorial. "They both had beautiful and interesting faces; but faces like Irving's have looked at the world for hundreds of years past from portraits of churchmen, statesmen, princes and saints, whilst Ellen's face had never been seen in the world before. She actually invented her own beauty; for her portraits as a girl have hardly anything in them of the wonderful woman who, after leaving the stage for seven years, reappeared in 1875 and took London by storm."

But Shaw admired intellect more than fire or brilliance in an actor: he preferred Duse to Bernhardt, and from much of his writing it would seem, Forbes-Robertson to Irving. Many admired Irving for the intellect behind his characterizations; but it was not a Shavian intellect, it was the intellect of an actor, not a thinker or a writer. Sir Johnston Forbes-Robertson was, like Macready and unlike Irving, a fine actor whose interest was not mainly in acting: the exact type of actor, in fact, Shaw was seeking for his own plays, and it was eventually Forbes-Robertson who created his Caesar. Perhaps for this reason he is at his finest on acting when writing of Forbes-Robertson's Hamlet, which he played at the Lyceum in the autumn of 1897 with Mrs. Patrick Campbell as Ophelia. And appreciation of the actor brought out in Shaw what we might tend from some of his statements to overlook: his considerable knowledge of the content of Shakespeare's plays and understanding of their finer points.

Mr. Forbes Robertson is essentially a classical actor, the only one, with the exception of Mr. Alexander, now established in London management. What I mean by classical is that he can present a dramatic hero as a man whose passions are those which have produced the philosophy, the poetry, the art, and the statecraft of the world, and not merely those which have produced its weddings, coroners' inquests, and executions. And that is just the sort of actor that Hamlet requires. . . . Hamlet is not a man in whom "common humanity" is raised by great vital energy to a heroic pitch, like Coriolanus or Othello. On the contrary, he is a man in whom the common personal passions are so superseded by wider and rarer interests, and so discouraged by a degree of critical self-consciousness which makes the practical efficiency of the instinctive man on the lower plane impossible to him, that he finds the duties dictated by conventional revenge and ambi-

tion as disagreeable a burden as commerce is to a poet. . . .
. . . please observe this is not a cold Hamlet. He is none of your logicians who reason their way through the world because they cannot feel their way through it: his intellect is the organ of his passion: his eternal self-criticism is as alive and thrilling as it can possibly be. The great soliloquy—no: I do NOT mean "To be or not to be": I mean the dramatic one, "O what a rogue and peasant slave am I!"—is as passionate in its scorn of brute passion as the most bull-necked affirmation or sentimental dilution of it could be. It comes out so without violence: Mr. Forbes Robertson takes the part quite easily and spontaneously. There is none of that strange Lyceum intensity which comes from the perpetual struggle between Sir Henry Irving and Shakespeare. The lines help Mr. Forbes Robertson instead of getting in his way at every turn, because he wants to play Hamlet, and not to slip into his inky cloak a changeling of quite another race. We may miss the craft, the skill double-distilled by constant peril, the subtlety, the dark rays of heat generated by intense friction, the relentless parental tenacity and cunning with which Sir Henry nurses his own pet creations on Shakespearean food like a fox rearing its litter in the den of a lioness; but we get light, freedom, naturalness, credibility and Shakespeare. It is wonderful how easily everything comes right when you have the right man with the right mind for it—how the story tells itself, how the characters come to life, how even the failures in the cast cannot confuse you, though they may disappoint you.

This is revealing not only of Forbes-Robertson's Hamlet but of Shakespeare's; a beautiful piece of criticism not shadowed by a brilliantly characteristic image of one of the performance's "failures," the Ghost of Forbes-Robertson's brother Ian: "The voice is not a bad voice; but it is the voice of a man who does not believe in ghosts. Moreover, it is a hungry voice, not that of one who is past eating."

In spite of his strange criticism elsewhere of Shakespeare's failure in character-drawing (partly, one suspects, because Shakespeare, though drawing all the emotions and psychological kinks of which the human race is capable, certainly by Shaw's standards omits reference in most cases to his characters' social views), Shaw, as in this case of Hamlet, sometimes shows a penetrating understanding of character of a kind one would not expect from his own plays. For instance, he describes Othello's jealousy as a "purely melodramatic jealousy," a criticism not unexpected from a man of Shaw's nature, and with some sense if one takes Iago's dubious motivation, and Othello's own early nobility, at their face value. But Shaw adds: "The real article is to be found later on in *A Winter's Tale,* where Leontes is an unmistakeable study of a jealous man from life."

Now this, with which few Shakespeare critics would agree, is a remarkably perspicacious observation. Leontes, once considered "theatrical" because apparently motiveless in his jealousy, and much inferior to Othello, is in the light of modern medical science a recognizable psychopath in his actions, his unreasoning passion, and the words in which he expresses his distorted and bitter physical images. His is a mind diseased, as most jealous minds are, and I agree with Shaw that the study is unmistakably drawn from life, as so much of the darker human passions are in these later plays of Shakespeare—*King Lear, Timon of Athens, A Winter's Tale,* the bitter comedies *Troilus and Cressida* and *All's Well That Ends Well,* even in fragments of *The Tempest*—where one feels a despair of humanity and an obsession about disloyalty and ingratitude: both qualities that could be associated in the jealous mind.

It is difficult to believe Shakespeare had not come into painful contact with such a mind, and felt the sting in particular of ingratitude; one play would prove nothing, half a dozen suggest something deeper and more personal than detached observation of life. It is strange that Shaw should see this in Leontes, much ahead of his time generally; and it argues his knowledge of human nature was clearer than a superficial view of his plays has suggested to some.

In fact Shaw's generalizations about Shakespeare, written from the point of view of one who could not in all reason be wholly impartial and detached, are offset by a thorough knowledge of the plays, as well as production and acting, which combine to make much of his Shakespearean criticism still not only readable but illuminating. His musical "ear" could hardly miss the splendors of the verse, and good speaking of it was something he continually clamored for, complaining of the lack of "the Shakespearean music" in Tree's production of *Julius Caesar*. "When we come to those unrivalled grandiose passages in which Shakespeare turns on the full organ, we want to hear the sixteen-foot pipes booming, or, failing them (as we often must, since so few actors are naturally equipped with them), the ennobled tone, and the tempo suddenly steadied with the majesty of deeper purpose. You have, too, those moments when the verse, instead of opening up the depths of sound, rises to its most brilliant clangor, and the lines ring like a thousand trumpets. If we cannot have these effects, or if we can only have genteel drawing-room arrangements of them, we cannot have Shakespeare."

His eye and sound stage sense made him an equally quick judge of production effects (he would obviously have made a good director himself, outside his own plays where actors soon discovered this). He notes of a production of *Othello:* "The storm, the dread of shipwreck, the darkness, the fierce riot, the 'dreadful bell that frights the isle from its propriety', are not only not suggested, but contradicted, by the scenery and management. We are shown a delightful Mediterranean evening; the bell is as pretty as an operatic angelus; Othello[3] comes in like a temperance lec-

[3] Wilson Barrett.

turer; Desdemona does not appear; and the exclamation,

'Look, if my gentle love be not raised up—
I'll make thee an example',

becomes a ludicrously schoolmasterly 'I'll make thee an example', twice repeated."

His understanding of acting as applied to character is reasoned in the best actor's sense as well as the author's. "Dogberry is a capital study of parochial character. Sincerely played, he always comes out as a very real and entertaining person. At the St. James's, I grieve to say, he does not carry a moment's conviction: he is a mere mouthpiece for malapropisms, all of which he shouts at the gallery with intense consciousness of their absurdity, and with open anxiety lest they should pass unnoticed. Surely it is clear, if anything histrionic is clear, that Dogberry's first qualification must be a complete unconsciousness of himself as he appears to others."

This criticism would bear repeating to many comedians playing Dogberry and like parts today. It pinpoints the essence of good comedy *character* playing, and shows Shaw's knowledge of acting technique and its problems as sharply as does his acute comment to Ellen Terry regarding Mrs. Warren's long speech to her daughter in his own play: "The real difficulty in that scene is not Mrs. Warren's talking, but Vivie's listening." Every actress would bear out the truth of this.

But just as Wagner's need tore from Shaw as an opera critic not only his crusading spirit but some of his finest music criticism, Ibsen's equal need in the world of drama sharpened his pen to his most illuminating analyses of plays. The fact that the plays were worthy the pen had, of course, a great deal to do with this: the best criticism is never wholly derogatory, and a great critic is at his greatest when writing of works which test his highest powers of mental and aesthetic understanding. Shaw's mind and Ibsen's were of similar metal, when struck giving out the same steely tone, the same flash of idea. The impact produced not only Shaw's sociological plays (in partial influence, at any rate, for his political work made their ultimate direction inevitable), but also the book of short essays on the plays, *The Quintessence of Ibsenism,* first published in 1891 before Ibsen had written his last plays, and revised to include the omissions in 1913.

It is here we see Shaw's own dramatic impulses being molded, even as with masterly conciseness he analyzes the work of another. On the surface these are brief summaries of plot and character, but the surface has a solid mental rock, not hollowness, beneath it. Much of the criticism still throws a beam of light on the plays, and is so well written that it is memorable in its own right. And Shaw is as good on the early symbolic dramas as the later realistic ones, giving its due to the noble tragedy of *Brand,* a play considered more or less unstageable in England until 1959, when the courageous young '59 Theatre Company at the Lyric Theatre, Hammersmith, under the artistic direction of Caspar Wrede with Michael Elliot as director, presented a version of the play which put it irrevocably in its place as a tremendously exciting and imaginative piece of theatre, with a performance of Brand by the remarkable young actor, Patrick McGoohan, which revealed the moving humanity, no less than the towering classical pride and power, of one of the greatest acting parts in heroic drama.

"Don Quixote, Brand, and Peer Gynt," wrote Shaw, "are, all three, men of action seeking to realize their ideals in deeds . . . Peer, selfish rascal as he is, is not unlovable. Brand, made terrible by the consequences of his idealism to others, is heroic. Their castles in the air are more beautiful than castles of brick and mortar; but one cannot live in them . . ."

It is often said that Shaw as a writer lacks imagination or poetry: a contention which cannot seriously be held by anyone capable of realizing the creative impulse behind

Saint Joan and *Back to Methuselah,* not to count a character such as Captain Shotover in *Heartbreak House.* What is certainly true is that as a critic he was fully capable of being fired by the imaginative work of others, and his appreciation of Ibsen—the Ibsen of the early poetic dramas and the later ones, in which realism yields once more to the drive of the symbolic—was by no means only sociological. His own phrase for the master—"the iron-mouthed Ibsen"—is a poetic one, great prose as in Shaw's case often molding itself imaginatively if not structurally into the tones and images of the poet.

He learned from the plays' craftsmanship, could assess it and in his own early plays use it; until he felt, as all individual artists do at one point in their career, the strength and ability to throw away their masters' books of rules and forge something fresh and original from the molten steel of their own minds. The supple torrent of Shaw's wit and multi-radiant knowledge and ideas burst through the dams of Ibsen's careful play construction; but not everyone noticed that the skeleton architecture was still there beneath the shining flood of discursive conversation. More than one director has found to his cost how difficult it is to "cut" Shaw or ignore his careful stage directions even as regards the setting of a room: for all are based on a very clear theatrical plan and the removal of one nail in the structure can bring some apparently minor edifice crashing later. Actors have found the same with regard to his published descriptions of a character; one ignores Shaw's directions only at peril.

A lot of this meticulous sense of stage construction he got from Ibsen, putting it to his own uses. Ibsen also showed him the way in converting some social matter into dramatic form, making the theatre for the first time a sounding board of ideas, ideals and practical human reforms. And although Shaw by nature never matched the great Norwegian in psychological insight into the unpredictable reactions, stresses and revelations of the individual human character, he was fully able to appreciate what Ibsen was doing here and could adapt in his turn into his own more mentally astringent terms. Ibsen would have understood Louis Dubedat as well as Shaw understood Gregers Werle.

"The busybody thus finds that people cannot be freed from their failings from without. They must free themselves," Shaw writes of *The Wild Duck,* distilling its psychological essence in two brief sentences. Knowing no artist, however universal, can entirely tear up his own roots, he is, too, practical enough to grasp a possible reason for the "strangeness" of the later plays to English audiences: "The extreme type of Norwegian, as depicted by Ibsen, imagines himself doing wonderful things, but does nothing. He dreams as no Englishman dreams . . . it is for this reason that *Rosmersholm* and *The Lady from the Sea* strike English audiences as more fantastic and less literal than *A Doll's House* and the plays in which the leading figures are men and women of action, though to a Norwegian there is probably no difference in this respect." Yet he is not too practical either to reject the genuine otherworldliness that seems inherent in these later dramas, and his preface to the four last plays shows a sensitivity to the spirit of their greatness and their style:

> Ibsen now lays down the complete task of warning the world against its idols and anti-idols, and passes into the shadow of death, or rather into the splendor of his sunset glory; for his magic is extraordinarily potent in these four plays, and his purpose more powerful. And yet the shadow of death is here; for all four, except *Little Eyolf,* are tragedies of the dead, deserted and mocked by the young who are still full of life.

The Quintessence of Ibsenism and *The Perfect Wagnerite* were two of a trilogy of long essays summing up Shaw's views. The first two works dealt specifically with the two artists who to him were the peak creators of new forms in drama and music. The third, *The Sanity of Art,* came in 1895 between the other two, and spanned aesthetics in general and his own values. They are the *belles-lettres* expression of critical ideas which during the same period threw up sparks from the pages of the weekly journals for which he wrote.

Shaw himself stressed that his criticism was not the "overnight" criticism demanded of the journalist on the London daily newspaper. Answering a magazine catechism in 1901, on the subject of journalism as a profession, he made the following remark, obviously deeply considered:

> Daily journalism, being beyond mortal strength and endurance, trains literary men to scamp their work. A weekly feuilleton is at least possible: I did one for ten years, taking all the pains I was capable of to get to the bottom of every sentence I wrote. . . . Ten years of such work was an apprenticeship which made me master of my profession. But it was not daily journalism. I could not have achieved its quality had I undertaken more than one feuilleton; and even that I could not have done without keeping myself up to the neck all the rest of the week in other activities; gaining other efficiencies and gorging myself with life and experience as well. My income as a journalist began in 1885 at £117 0s. 3d.; and it ended at about £500, by which time I had reached the age at which we discover that journalism is a young man's standby, not an old man's livelihood. So, I conclude, even weekly journalism is superhuman except for young men. The older ones must scamp it; and the younger ones must live plainly and cheaply, if they are to get their authority up to the pitch at which they are allowed to say what they think. Of course, they do nothing of the sort. If they did, journalism would train them in literature as nothing else could. Would, but doesn't. It spoils them instead. If you want a problem stated, a practised journalist will do it with an air that is the next best thing to solving it. But he never solves it: he hasn't time, and wouldn't get paid any more for the solution if he

had time. So he chalks up the statement, and runs away from the solution.

Much of this is as true today as when Shaw practiced journalism. Genuine integrity and saying what he really thinks are still rarely possible to the reviewer on a daily paper, at the mercy of the sub-editor to a larger or lesser degree, and in some notorious cases to managerial policy—either political or for sensational overstatement. Shaw's unshakeable integrity caused him to resign one critical post as we have seen, and he never allowed himself to be trapped into writing a review without time for thought or reflection. Money was the last consideration (and even today, to write intelligent criticism under Shaw's conditions, the critic must usually accept less than a reasonable livelihood, for the journals of the highest literary standing are still the most restricted in readership and therefore payments).

Today we suffer from a lack of the more profound and knowledgeable criticism not only because the daily critic's views (presented, in England, in ludicrously restricted space) are given a notoriety and authority out of all proportion to their merit, while those of more serious writers on the weekly literary journals are much less widely read and disseminated; but also because, as I have said, critics of all kinds have had their range of understanding narrowed by specialization on one subject. The appreciation of plays, either of ideas or character, is dependent on as wide an experience of social or intellectual thought, and of human nature, as that possessed by the dramatist. A failure in criticism is partly a failure in living, and what so often divides the critic from the creator in the arts. Perhaps this is why the greatest critics rarely stay permanently or solely in criticism, or within the bounds of one subject.

Shaw was a great critic because he had within himself the seeds of creation, and the capacity to pitch his thought and experience of life alongside—not *against*—those of Wagner and Ibsen in their respective spheres. In the committee room, on the public-speaking platform, in the hurly-burly of politics and social reform, as well as—to a lesser, experimental but perhaps as necessary a degree—in my lady's chamber, he was, as he says, "gorging" himself "with life and experience," just as in the libraries, art galleries and museums, in the concert halls, opera houses and theatres, he was extending the frontiers of his mind to include every form of culture open to the educated man of his period.

With his natural wit and mental endowments there came, therefore, inevitably a time when criticism of the work of others could not proceed beyond a certain point without repetition and deadness of purpose. And in 1898, when he ceased regular criticism, his own first volume of plays—*Plays Pleasant and Unpleasant*—was published. He was, in fact, already acting on what he wrote and the interest he aroused as a dramatist was overlapping that which he aroused as a critic.

He never ceased to write criticism, in some sense or another, to the end of his days; but it was not, after 1898, as a regular paid reviewer of other people's plays. It was as a dramatist he finally made his mark on the world; and this was only in keeping with the vast resources and essential originality of his mind. It was a mind which in the end must produce its own vision of life, not reflect merely that of others; and because he was always a practical critic, interested in and constantly analyzing the technical processes (as music critic he had produced almost a small thesis on methods of piano-playing technique), it was inevitable that he would soon, like Wagner, start putting his ideas on stage reform into practice. There were plenty of social and political abuses which Ibsen had left undramatized; and if Ibsen was the creative spring releasing Shaw's own dramatic energies, Shaw was himself no less a genius of the written word with a hundred more public and human wrongs singing in his mind for redress.

Ibsen, more than anyone, taught him to use dramatic tools for the purpose. After that, the field was his own; and remained so, without rival, for over half a century.

Chapter 5

Ellen Terry

SHAW'S WRITING WAS not all professional; he was all his life, given the right responding mind, a brilliant and fluent letterwriter, able to establish a *rapport* of personality which argues that his sensitivity to human character—and ability to provoke it to reveal itself on paper—was more pronounced than many might realize.

His correspondence with the actress Ellen Terry began in 1892, when she wrote to his editor Edmund Yates about a singer protégé she would like the music critic of *The World* to hear. Shaw answered her personally, but only his second letter survives, following his visit to her young friend's recital. Thereafter the correspondence developed into something that Shaw, prefacing the correspondence when it was published after her death in 1928, described frankly as "a paper courtship, which is perhaps the pleasantest, as it is the most enduring, of all courtships."

It spanned, at its height, all the years of Shaw's professional work as a critic and his earliest work as a playwright; indeed in a sense it is a bridge between the two, although for a time he practiced both professions simultaneously. It is illuminating and important in any study of Shaw; not only in supplementing his official theatre criticisms, including advice to Ellen on interpretation and production which she was intelligent enough to recognize as just, and often acted upon; but in throwing a light, sometimes directly, more often by implication, on his creative work and the processes of his mind and emotions.

In a sense, although he was slow to admit it, Ellen Terry threw around him, as she threw around all men, a veil of femininity and grace and kindness of heart that was essentially romantic in its enchantment. But this would not, with Shaw, have bound him for two days had she not also, as he early discovered, had a mind of her own which, unlike her partner Irving's, flowered in contact with wit, thought, people and interests entirely outside the theatre.

One of a famous acting family, she grew up into the theatre by force of circumstance; but her arranged marriage at fifteen years old to a famous and much older painter, G. F. Watts, had early developed in her a sensitivity to and knowledge of art, to which she added, as life heightened her responses, a wider education, a spontaneous talent for description and analysis in writing, and a natural and warmly-dispensed wisdom. "One of the greatest letter-writers that ever lived," Shaw described her in the *Neue Freie Presse* of Vienna; "she can flash her thought down on paper in a handwriting that is as characteristic and unforgettable as her face."

When reaching her height as a young actress she threw up her career without hesitation or regret in order to keep house in the country on £3 a week for the man she most deeply loved, the distinguished Victorian architect Edward William Godwin. Godwin provided her with two adored and talented children, Edith and Edward Gordon Craig, but was not able to marry her and apparently left them to be supported by her. It was to do this that she accepted an offer from Irving and returned to acting six years later. "Irving," as Shaw succinctly pointed out, "would not have left the stage for a night to spend it with Helen of Troy."

It was this mental and emotional cleavage between Ellen Terry and Irving that, with the accident of the correspondence and his own strong position as widely-read critic on *The Saturday Review*, Shaw made small bones about emphasizing: consciously with the hope (which must very soon have dimmed) of arousing Irving's sense of responsibility towards the new drama, subconsciously, there seems little doubt if one reads between the lines, in a personal exasperation that the radiant and talented Ellen should not only subdue her own genius to play "second fiddle" to Irving in his stage projects, but give her heart and loyalty as a woman to him as well.

Shaw in his preface to the correspondence flatters himself that he did in the end open Ellen's eyes to her real position at the Lyceum and drive a wedge between her and Irving—too late, he admits, for she was now at the age difficult to cast in leading roles and her notorious lack of concentration had permanently affected her memory of her lines. But the truth is, it was not so much that Ellen Terry gave up the Lyceum as that the Lyceum itself gave up both Ellen and Irving. A series of financial losses on productions, and a disastrous fire in which he lost stage scenery and properties accumulated over twenty years of management, sent Irving in his waning years on provincial and foreign tours, unable any longer to cope with the expenses and responsibilities of London production; and Ellen herself was already growing beyond the age for her accepted Shakespearean parts.

She was never, as Shaw noted, a versatile actress, though "soundly skilled in the technique of her profession," he wrote: "the spectators would have resented it: they did not want Ellen Terry to be Olivia Primrose:[1] they wanted Olivia Primrose to be Ellen Terry. Her combination of beauty with sensitive intelligence was unique: a disguise would have been intolerable. Her instinct was for beauty and for sincerity: she had only to play a part 'straight,' as actors say, to transfigure it into something much better than its raw self."

Moreover, to Ellen's own distress, a rift had fallen between herself and Irving in later years which was not on her own part and was unexplained, yet potent, on his. A re-

[1] In Goldsmith's *The Vicar of Wakefield*, one of the most popular of Irving's productions at the Lyceum.

served man fanatically devoted to and absorbed in his art, he seems, as his grandson Laurence in his penetrating *Life* suggests, to have come as near to loving Ellen Terry as he was capable of loving any woman beyond and outside his work in the theatre. Laurence even suggests, more disputably, that it was Ellen herself who foresaw the disaster in which a divorce and marriage to her would involve him, a preëminent actor who had gained for his profession a hardwon recognition in respectable Victorian society: she therefore refused him. It does not sound like Ellen, who when she gave her heart did so without thought of convention; but Irving, a solitary man with a broken and unsuitable marriage, subtly retired into his shell: perhaps (who can tell?) unsure of her real feelings, perhaps thinking better of it for the sake of his career and his responsibilities to his profession and the many people dependent on him at the Lyceum Theatre. He remained scrupulously polite to her in society, and unbridgeably distant; and she, who certainly loved him deeply as the friend and fellow-worker of many years, and much, it is obvious, for his own personal fascination too, suffered accordingly.

Of this suffering, and of this feeling for Irving generally, Shaw was certainly aware. He was not the man to express spite, but the correspondence is not devoid of its glimmers of jealousy, the jealousy being as much professional, of course, as personal; for there was no personal contact sought or given between Shaw and Ellen Terry, who as the correspondence progressed had their own intimate relationships elsewhere. Shaw's concern was with his own plays and Ibsen's and the possibility of Ellen, if not Irving himself as he had once dreamed, being able to act in them, as well as with genuine critical regret at what he considered her wasted talents at the Lyceum.

Nevertheless, he was on paper entranced, and so no less at times was she; they played tentatively with ideas of meeting, and perhaps destroying their illusions; and when she caught a glimpse of him when they were both, by accident, in the audience at the same play—six years after the correspondence began—she was not slow to tell him so: "I saw all your, so charmingly disguised, yawns during (and between) the acts. . . . You have the 'youngest' look I ever saw on any animal's face except Fussy's! I should like to go about with you for you are so quiet, with pauses, in your chatter."

Fussy was Henry Irving's beloved dog, and it is doubtful if Shaw relished this comparison. But the reference to his youthfulness—which one feels she meant as much to apply to his expression and personality as to looks—is characteristic of her. She was eight years his senior, and with all men her feelings and instincts tended to be maternal to some degree, the capacity for sympathy, compassion and protectiveness springing not infrequently from her practical wisdom and understanding of life. It was a quality Shaw recognized in her, and from which in part (though he denied it in later years) he created Candida in her likeness. What she saw, apart from the chameleon personality and brilliant critic on paper whom she already knew, was a tall, thin Irishman of forty-one, dressed defiantly for the theatre in the unconventional tweeds that so shocked the susceptibilities of the socially correct Irving, with shrewd, blue, humorous eyes, bushy eyebrows jerked upwards like those of an operatic Mephistopheles, and a titian-red beard that elongated the narrow head until it seemed like that of some mischievous Satan whom El Greco had unaccountably omitted to oppose on canvas to the figure of his Christ.

It is obvious she liked what she saw, but they did not seriously meet until rehearsals of *Captain Brassbound's Conversion* at the Court Theatre years later, when at last Shaw had succeeded in capturing her for a leading part in his play. His account of the meeting is entertaining, for it provided full scope for his sense of anticlimax in humor.

By that time Irving had passed out of her life, and indeed out of his own; and Ellen's heart was for the moment vacant. I could not help speculating as to the possibility of my filling the vacancy. But Providence had other views. At our first serious meeting in the rehearsal room at the Court Theatre, Ellen and I were talking together before business began when the door opened, and a young American actor, James Carew, who had been engaged to play the part of Captain Hamlin Kearney, came in. "Who is that?" said Ellen, looking at him with quick interest. "That's the American captain," I answered. Without an instant's hesitation she sailed across the room; put Mr. Carew in her pocket (so to speak); and married him.[2] The lucky captive naturally made no resistance, though I cannot believe that James had any choice of his own in the matter. I was awestruck; for I had not believed it possible for even the most wonderful of women to choose her man at a single glance and bear him off before he had time to realize who she was. Shooting a lion at sight is child's play in comparison, because it does not matter which lion it happens to be: If you do not kill it, it may kill you; so—bang! But it matters very much which man it is when marriage is in question; and so swift a decision by a huntress who, far from being promiscuous in her attachments, was highly fastidious, made me marvel and say to myself "There, but for the grace of God, goes Bernard Shaw."

Carew was many years Ellen Terry's junior, as her first husband, Watts, had been many years older; but though neither marriage proved lasting she retained the warm friendship of both men afterwards, as Shaw says. His own regard for her, and sense of her magic, never left him. She died blind at the age of eighty, still radiant, still serene.

[2] The marriage actually took place during an American tour at Pittsburgh a year later, on March 22, 1907. But the pocketing was doubtless almost as swift as Shaw said, for Ellen had fabulous charm.

And in June, 1929, a year later, Shaw was still able to end his preface to their letters with two of the most touching sentences he ever wrote:

> She became a legend in her old age; but of that I have nothing to say; for we did not meet, and, except for a few broken letters, did not write; and she never was old to me.
>
> Let those who may complain that it was all on paper remember that only on paper has humanity yet achieved glory, beauty, truth, knowledge, virtue, and abiding love.

Chapter 6

The Establishment of the Dramatist

"DRAMA," SHAW ONCE wrote, "is no mere setting up of the camera to nature; it is the presentation in parable of the conflict between man's will and his environment; in a word, of problem."

No one who cannot grasp this can hope to appreciate fully Shaw's plays. Like Ibsen, he was realist only on the surface; his realistic problems were presented not in photographic terms but through the heightened symbols of dramatic speech and sociological or philosophical or economic idea. No dramatist before or since (certainly not Ibsen, whose psychological stresses and subtleties threw, in the end, a more illuminating and lasting beam on human nature than its social environment) has used prose dialogue with such care and elaboration to embody, not his characters' private feelings, but their public and private motives, prejudices and levels of thought. They are pillars of society and as such brought into being both to promote reforms and to entertain; for as playwright no less than lecturer and critic Shaw knew, none better, that a first essential in winning an argument and presenting a point of view was to gain and (harder) keep the interest of an audience.

His weapon was comedy because he knew it was the strongest he possessed, but it did not deflect his basic seriousness of purpose. "Many things of which I have made fun in my plays will be made tragedy by future playwrights," he wrote. And no critic falls into a wider trap than the one who assumes from this that Shaw's characters are not drawn from human nature as he had experienced it, or leavened by some of the yeast of the writer's creative imagination.

"I am not governed by principles; I am inspired, how or why I cannot explain, because I do not know; but inspiration it must be; for it comes to me without reference to my own ends or interests." We can be quite sure that when Shaw wrote this he was no more humbugging the public or himself than Wagner was when he described the half-waking dream of drowning that provided the inspiration for the Prelude to *Das Rheingold*. For whole passages in *Heartbreak House, Saint Joan* and *Back to Methuselah* confirm it. It is always necessary to bear this pure inspiration in mind, and make allowance for it, in assessing Shaw's plays, as it is necessary to realize that his characters are not the less real because they strip away what an excellent critic, C. B. Purdom, has called the "romantic pretenses" that until Shaw's time, and to some extent still today, so often form a kind of fictional veil around *dramatis personae* in the theatre.

Characteristically, Shaw was one of the first to eliminate that Latin inscription from his characters, and to write plays for entertaining reading in which the technical jargon is replaced by preliminary and incidental descriptions of scene and character. To him, if a play was good enough to be seen in the theatre it was good enough to be read by the large body of the public which for moral or other reaons was unable or unwilling to visit the playhouse. But if his descriptive matter was aimed at the reading public—forcing many of them for the first time to accept modern drama as good literature—it was also meant as a guide to the actor and director, which both have often found they ignore at their peril.

Nevertheless a statement he wrote for the Censorship Committee in 1909 is essentially true: "I am a specialist in unmoral and heretical plays. My reputation has been gained by my persistent struggle to force the public to reconsider its morals. . . ." And by morals, of course, he means not erotic behavior but matters of individual and public conscience, whole systems of society and narrow-minded or conservative thinking. He abused these things not so much for their own sakes as for the appalling human tragedies of poverty, warped mentalities and suffering they caused. Until Ibsen the public platform and press, not the theatre, had been the only accepted channels for such propaganda and advocacy of reforms; and to these Shaw had automatically turned to express his views, with an unsuccessful attempt to use fictional means through the novel, as Tolstoy had done.

It is curious that not even Ibsen, for whom he continually beat a critical drum, seems to have given Shaw the idea of using the stage as a platform: his humility was greater than any of his enemies ever realized (or themselves practiced), and his deep admiration and understanding of Ibsen's plays as works of genius if anything probably held him back. To the end, in one or two revealing statements, he acknowledged that the irresistible Joey in him (as his comic spirit came to be called after Mrs. Patrick Campbell's nickname for him) destroyed his own chances to earn the title of a "great" writer.

It was, in fact, William Archer, as I have previously mentioned, who first turned his mind towards playwriting by proposing they should collaborate in writing a play: "he," as Shaw later explanied, "to supply the constructional scaffolding or scenario, and I to fill in the dialogue." But Archer's innate romanticism (apparently undeflected in his own writing by Ibsen, in spite of his championship and translation of the Norwegian's plays), and Shaw's lively astringency of mind, came inevitably into conflict over the development of the story: immovable block met immovable block, and the first two acts of what was to become *Widowers' Houses* were abandoned, apparently without regret, by both parties.

It was J. T. Grein, founder in 1891 of the new Independent Theatre as a revolutionary English channel for the plays of Ibsen, who in 1892 was instrumental in turning Shaw into a professional dramatist. Shaw felt that his theatre, if it was to have any lasting influence on the English stage, was urgently in need of new plays by new national dramatists, and that he himself might fulfill the requirement. Shaw made the suggestion to Grein in a long walk which began in the Hammersmith Road at midnight and ended many hours later, in early morning: a marathon as memorable in history as its prototype in an earlier civilization. For the end of it was that Shaw proposed, for the purpose of bridging Grein's dramatic gap, to resurrect the play he had so transformed from Archer's original idea in 1885, and complete it with a third act.

Widowers' Houses, as he called it, was presented by the Independent Theatre Society at the Royalty Theatre in London on December 9, 1892, with a repeat performance on December 13. "The first performance was sufficiently exciting," wrote Shaw in his Preface to the published edition; "the Socialists and Independents applauded me furiously on principle; the ordinary playgoing first-nighters hooted me frantically on the same ground; I, being at that time in some practice as what is impolitely called a mob orator, made a speech before the curtain; the newspapers discussed the play for a whole fortnight. . . . I had not achieved a success; but I had provoked an uproar; and the sensation was so agreeable that I resolved to try again."

The result was *The Philanderer*, a comedy which Shaw, already a practiced judge of acting technique, soon realized was beyond the scope of the Independent Theatre. "I had written a part which nobody but Charles Wyndham could act, in a play which was impossible at his theatre." The play, written in 1893, was therefore shelved until 1905, when it was presented briefly by the New Stage Club, though its first public performances did not occur until

1907 at the Royal Court Theatre under the Vedrenne-Barker management.

In the meantime, during 1893 and 1894, Shaw wrote *Mrs. Warren's Profession*, which also could not be produced by the Independent Theatre because it was realized, quite correctly, that the English Censor, the Lord Chamberlain, would ban it. It was, in fact, presented in London by a private club, the Stage Society, in 1902, six years later, and in spite of public performances in the United States (at the Hyperion Theatre, New Haven, Connecticut, and Garrick Theatre, New York, by Arnold Daly, in October and November, 1905) it did not in fact receive a public London production until September 28, 1925, when it was presented by the Macdona Players in repertory at the Regent Theatre, King's Cross. This was followed by a new production and run of sixty-five performances at the Strand Theatre beginning on March 3, 1926: almost exactly a quarter of a century after its genesis.

This is the trilogy of plays grouped under the epithet "Unpleasant" in the first published volume of Shaw's plays, *Plays Pleasant and Unpleasant*, which appeared in 1898. And their production history, allied to the history of Shaw's novels and their rejection by publishers, makes it obvious that there was some bitter creative as well as pecuniary experience behind his reply, in 1901 when he was nearly forty-five years old, to a magazine question about his first real success: "Never had any. Success, in that sense, is a thing that comes to you, and takes your breath away, as it came to Byron and Dickens and Kipling. What came to me was repeated failure. By the time I wore it down I knew too much to care about either failure or success."

It is said first works of fiction are nearly always autobiographical; and although this cannot truly be said of Shaw's plays, there is no doubt not only his personal beliefs and moral indignations, but also his personal friendships, are reflected in them. This is true, of course, of all his plays to an extent; but in 1892 his early private and emotional affairs were still close to him, and the women from whom he had gained his experience of life, in particular, still vivid in this thoughts. We can therefore find here a special application of his later admonition to a biographer: ". . . you do not seem to make any allowance for the considerable part of a playwright's *dramatis personae* which consists in studies from the living model. Some of my characters are close portraits; for others I have used a model just as a painter does. You write throughout as if all my characters were allegorical personifications, not persons."

He is speaking particularly of Julia Craven in *The Philanderer:* "as much a study of jealousy as Leontes in *The Winter's Tale*," he wrote. And Julia, like Blanche Sartorius in his first play, with her decisive character, rages and animal sexual undercurrents, was based on the Jenny Paterson who had managed to captivate and hold him so long in his first affair. He himself, of course, was the model for the philanderer, Charteris, caught between the furious recriminations of the old love and the new; and it is because of its basis in a red-hot (for Shaw) personal experience that the first act of *The Philanderer* still seems so vital and strangely contemporary today. Its shattering of sex shibboleths and the accepted play "situations" at the time must have been startling: its honesty about people and their behavior in sexual relationships (and Shaw did not spare Charteris any more than the women—all his life he was as honest about himself as others) has survived its more ephemeral bantering of the "new woman" and the Ibsen Club.

It should be added that Grace Tranfield, the third character in the triangle, was based on Shaw's actress friend Florence Farr, and the scene between the two women—amusingly disgraceful enough!—was actually reproduced from an encounter between Shaw's Jenny and Florence.

This, indeed, was carrying Nora's rebellion in *A Doll's House*—an economic and intellectual rather than sexual one—several steps further; and though the character of Blanche in *Widowers' Houses* is not so important a point in the play, which was aimed at the enormities of slum ownership and exploitation, here too was a realistic, unromanticized honesty about a certain type of woman, stalking her man, that brought out into the open what had still been only implicit in the new drama. The Life Force, in fact, already had its clutches, through Blanche, on Dr. Harry Trench, although Shaw did not yet name it as such.

Widowers' Houses indeed burst a bomb in another direction, for it was aimed at what was then, and still is, the most sacred cow in the English social religion: private property. For this reason it is surprisingly apposite in some ways to the London of 1961, where homeless families were walking the streets—in spite of a so-called affluent society—for want of accommodation, and others, white and colored, were crowded into single rooms let at high rents by landlords in overcrowded slums. It was on the same principle that Sartorius let out his Victorian slum properties at rents of 4s. 6d. a room for a whole family, because the houses let out piecemeal in this way drew higher aggregate rents than if let as a whole or by the floor. It is the same principle, too, that makes it almost impossible for single people in London today to obtain accommodation comprising one room, kitchenette and bathroom, as they can in New York and almost any other European capital city, except at a fabulous rent far beyond the means of the average worker or secretary: scarcity value and the lure of high profits once again having encouraged landlords to let out their houses room by room, often hardly bigger than the divan-bed it contains, with communal bathrooms, no heating except at high extra cost, and no cooking facilities except by means of a small gas-ring—each of such rooms commanding a high rent and high profit in the aggregate, without providing the barest needs of truly civilized twentieth-century living.

There is, in fact, no such thing as a play permanently outdated on sociological grounds. Civilization is not, as idealists with small knowledge of history like to imagine, continuously progressive but retrograde according to circumstances even within a matter of fifty years. And although the worst conditions of slum living have been controlled to some extent by local government inspection and regulations, the license still exists in many areas for inadequate and insanitary conditions (in Glasgow, for instance). In London, unlike New York, a city which to its honor provides legislation to protect its inhabitants from the worst forms of exploitation, there is no obligation on the landlord to provide central heating, or indeed any adequate heating of any kind. In fact central heating still does not exist in the average home, and where it does exist, in luxury apartments and luxury hotels, it is inadequate without the aid of an electric or gas fire maintained at the tenant's cost.

As a result thc English poor and aged, those in fact who have not shared in the advantages of higher wages and the welfare state, sit in thousands of cases throughout the winter totally or partially in the cold, while the rest—in a society where wages are still one half or one third of those in the United States, and rents in London now almost or absolutely as high—only pay for their warmth out of money which might provide them with leisure, culture, or other comforts, including food.

To American readers this will seem difficult to imagine, for although they have slums of their own, the landlord in New York who does not provide certain minimum comforts, including free central heating, can be brought into Court and fined. But an understanding of it is necessary if they, and the high-salaried executives who alone in England enjoy better conditions, are to realize why *Widowers'*

Houses today is not "dated" by its subject, but merely a period aspect of an abuse of capitalist society which persists in a not very different form. Its true basis is character; the wealth of the world's Sartoriuses being garnered from a harvest of greed, indifference to, and exploitation of others, while many who, like Harry Trench, think themselves shocked and immune find that they, too, derive benefits indirectly, and are therefore responsible in the eyes of society. The average man, like Trench at the end of this play, learns to shut his eyes and ask no more questions. "I'm All Right, Jack" is a theme of Shaw's late Victorian play no less than of the Boulting Brothers' satirical postwar film. It was a cynical, realist and deliberately antiromantic conclusion, shocking to his period cushioned on romantic idealization in the theatre; but it was also an honest one, and in this Shaw began as he meant to go on.

If *Mrs. Warren's Profession* "dates" more in one way, it is because Shaw here bases his thesis on what a more generally affluent postwar society has found to be a fallacy: that prostitution, or brothel-keeping, Mrs. Warren's profession, is primarily the result of poverty and appallingly low women's wages, in fact the "sweat shop" and the subjugation of women. In the English welfare state, as we know, crime and vice have flourished like the green bay tree, and it has become obvious that many women like the life, and prefer it with its profits and freedom to hard work: a fact that Shaw, romantic in this one particular—blindness to the sexual urge in women, and also laziness, as additional motives for profit—did not look squarely in the face.

He was, perhaps, still nearer the mark than some care to accept, in that he was partly right; if even in an age of apparent plenty, as we have seen, many suffer from too high rents and lack of adequate homes, it is also true that women in England are, by male standards, still underpaid and limited in choice of professions, especially older women (female factory wages, for instance, average half those of male workers). A certain number of women who haven't a man to depend on as a permanent bread-winner are still therefore tempted to the more lucrative, easier way of life by economic factors. But it is not the full picture, and indeed Shaw in his character-drawing of Mrs. Warren shows himself implicitly aware of the fact that the type of woman—in this case a woman of a certain coarseness of fibre—counts no less than economic necessity.

In fact, *Mrs. Warren's Profession* reads blazingly well today, mainly through its excellent construction (it is, in its revelations, closer than many plays Shaw wrote to the "well-made play") and its character-drawing. Vivie, the matter-of-fact, scholastic, "new woman" daughter, is a genuine study (Shaw admitted her smoking was based on that of the real life person on whom she was modeled) and her difference from her mother, in natural temperament, education and outlook, provides the living human conflict of the play and keeps it strongly alive.

Mrs. Warren herself is depicted as coarse yet full of the feeling Vivie lacks. It is the kind of feeling, fairly shallow, by which Shaw does not set great store, but nevertheless portrays with compassion and skill. It is a clever and believable study and every scene in which Mrs. Warren appears has a flesh-and-blood reality. The hint of a potential unrealized incest between Vivie Warren and Frank seems to owe something to Ibsen's *Ghosts*, just as Lickcheese in *Widowers' Houses* owes something, almost certainly, to Pancks, the rent collector in Dickens' *Little Dorrit*.

Professionally, however, as we have seen, these first plays—two of them unperformable or unperformed—did little to establish Shaw as a dramatist, and it was not until the famous joint management of J. E. Vedrenne and Granville-Barker at the Royal Court Theatre began in 1904 that Shaw's plays were produced well enough and in sufficient quantity for his name to become a force in the theatre

Fig. 1. ELLEN TERRY. From the painting by her first husband, G. F. Watts.
(By permission of the National Portrait Gallery, London)

Fig. 2. MRS. PATRICK CAMPBELL (STELLA) in *Mr. and Mrs. Daventry*. *(Photo lent by Radio Times Hulton Picture Library, London)*

Fig. 3. MRS. SHAW (CHARLOTTE). Pastel portrait by Sartorio, over the mantelpiece of the drawing room at Shaw's Corner, Ayot St. Lawrence. *(Photo by Keystone Press, London. Lent by The National Trust, London)*

Fig. 4. "CORNO DI BASSETTO," early 1890's. *(Photo lent by Camera Press, London)*

Fig. 5. THE YOUNG BERNARD SHAW, c. 1880, aged twenty-four. *(Photo lent by Radio Times Hulton Picture Library, London)*

Fig. 6. T. E. LAWRENCE ("LAWRENCE OF ARABIA"). *(Photo by Howard Coster, London)*

Fig. 7. SHAW'S STUDY at his house, Shaw's Corner, Ayot St. Lawrence. *(Photo lent by The National Trust, London)*

Fig. 8. SHAW'S HOUSE (back view from garden), Shaw's Corner, Ayot St. Lawrence. *(Photo lent by The National Trust, London)*

Fig. 9. GRANVILLE BARKER as Frank in *Mrs. Warren's Profession,* Stage Society production, 1902

Fig. 10. SHAW REHEARSING LILLAH McCARTHY as Lavinia in the first production of *Androcles and the Lion,* 1913. *(Photo from Victoria & Albert Museum, London)*

Fig. 11. MAN AND SUPERMAN—1905. Act I. Original London production, Royal Court Theatre. Granville Barker as John Tanner and Lillah McCarthy as Ann Whitefield. *(Photo from Victoria & Albert Museum, London)*

Fig. 12. MAN AND SUPERMAN—1951. Don Juan in Hell scene, Act III. Revival, New Theatre, London. John Clements as Don Juan and Kay Hammond as Donna Anna. *(Photo by Houston Rogers, London)*

Fig. 13. MAJOR BARBARA, Act III. Revival, Old Vic, 1935. Maurice Evans as Adolphus Cusins, the Professor of Greek. *(Photo by J. W. Debenham, London)*

Fig. 14. HEARTBREAK HOUSE. Revival, Cambridge Theatre, London, 1943. Robert Donat as Captain Shotover. *(Photo by John Vickers)*

Fig. 15. SYBIL THORNDIKE as Saint Joan. Rheims Cathedral scene, first London production, 1924, New Theatre. *(Photo by The Times, London)*

Fig. 16. THE APPLE CART, first London production, 1929, Queens Theatre, with Edith Evans as Orinthia and Cedric Hardwicke as King Magnus. *(Photo by Sasha. Lent by Radio Times Hulton Picture Library, London)*

Fig. 17. CYRIL CUSACK as Androcles in Shaw Centenary production of *Androcles and the Lion,* Gaiety Theatre, Dublin, 1956

Fig. 18. CYRIL CUSACK as Bluntschli in *Arms and the Man,* Paris Festival production, 1960, won international critics' award for Best Acting Performance at the Festival. *(Photo by Studio Lipnitzki, Paris)*

Fig. 19. ARMS AND THE MAN, Act I. Scene with Cyril and Maureen Cusack as Bluntschli and Raina, Paris Festival production, 1960. *(Photo by Studio Lipnitzki, Paris)*

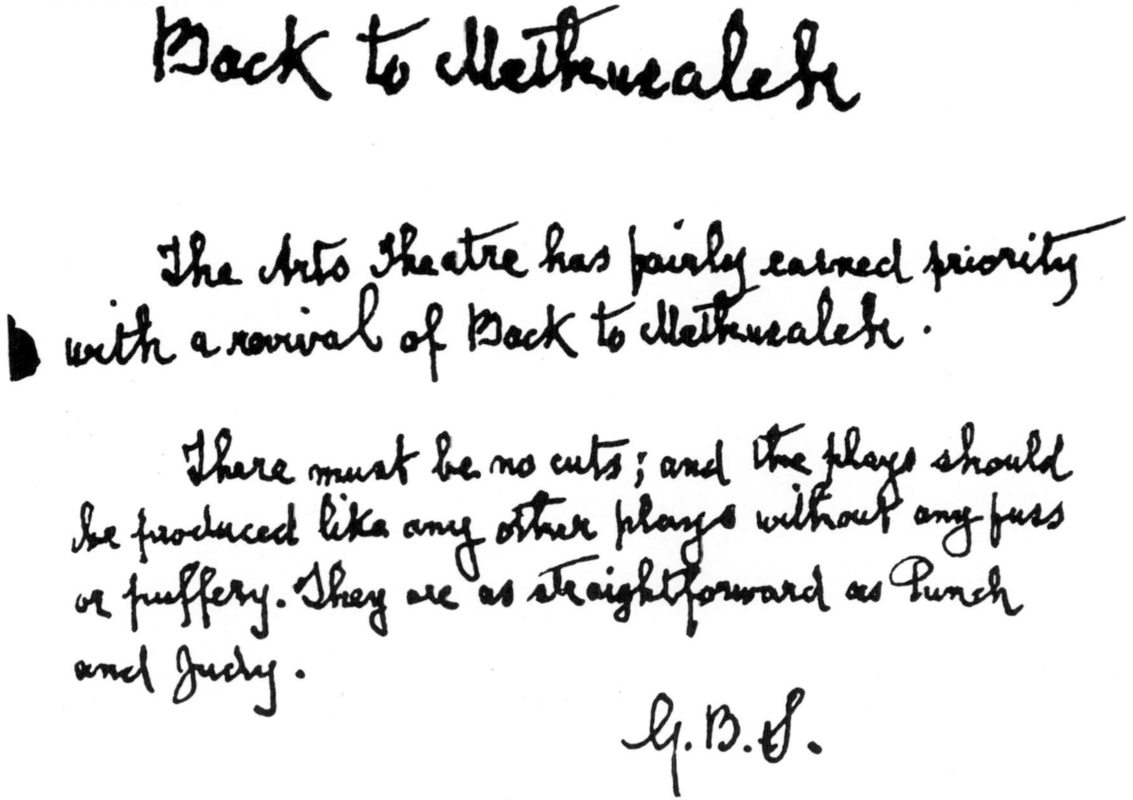

Back to Methusaleh

The Arts Theatre has fairly earned priority with a revival of Back to Methusaleh.

There must be no cuts; and the plays should be produced like any other plays without any fuss or puffery. They are as straightforward as Punch and Judy.

G.B.S.

Fig. 20. FACSIMILE POSTCARD in Shaw's handwriting giving permission to the Arts Theatre, London, to revive *Back to Methuselah* in full, 1947 (Note Shaw's spelling: Methusaleh) *(Photo by John Vickers)*

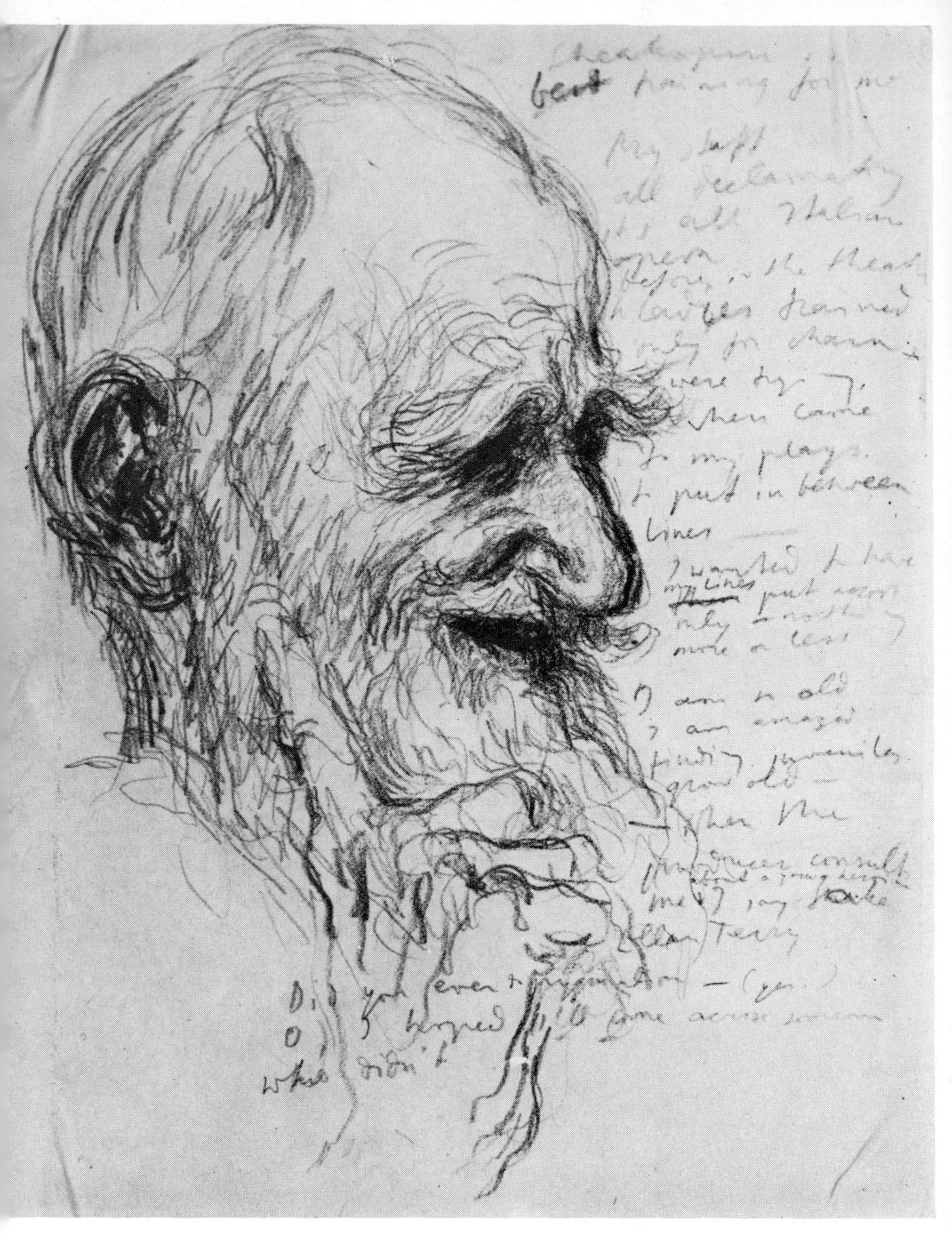

Fig. 21. SHAW drawn by Topolski, February, 1944, with pencil notes in Shaw's handwriting. *(Photo lent by Radio Times Hulton Picture Library, London)*

Fig. 22. SHAW, aged sixty-eight, January, 1925. *(Photo lent by Radio Times Hulton Picture Library, London)*

Fig. 23. THE ELDER SHAW, June, 1948, aged ninety-one. *(Photo by Karsh of Ottawa. Lent by Camera Press, London)*

as a writer of the highest quality, whose plays could also be counted a success with the public. But in the meantime he not only continued writing, but owing to the formation in 1899 of the Stage Society—a club able to function before a private audience of its members without the Lord Chamberlain's license—gained production of most of his earliest plays, even though on a limited scale.

The Society was founded "to give performances of plays of obvious power and merit which lacked, under the conditions then prevalent on the stage, any opportunity for their presentation," and its opening production (on November 26, 1899) was Shaw's *You Never Can Tell,* followed by *Candida* and *Captain Brassbound's Conversion* (1900), *Mrs. Warren's Profession* (1902), *The Admirable Bashville* (1903), *Man and Superman* (1905), *The Shewing-Up of Blanco Posnet* (1910), *Augustus Does His Bit* (1917), *O'Flaherty, V.C.* (1920) and (at last!) *Widowers' Houses* (1931, at the Malvern Festival). Nearly all were first performances, and although two or three were short unimportant plays it will be seen the list includes several of Shaw's most famous works, later performed with genuine public success at the Court Theatre under the Barker management.

The list excludes several important plays not produced at the Court either, including *Arms and the Man,* which followed *Mrs. Warren's Profession* in 1894. It was staged by Florence Farr, in association with Miss Horniman, founder of England's famous first repertory company at Manchester, at the Avenue Theatre in London, where it ran for fifty performances. Florence herself played Louka, the pert but shrewd-minded and independent Bulgarian maid, who was Shaw's own characteristic transportation of the "new woman" from high or professional society into the peasant class (that human beings were fundamentally equal and capable of absorbing social ideas and liberties irrespective of class was a part of his philosophy so innate to him that he scarcely bothered to comment on it—though then as now, in spite of lip service to democracy, society by no means always accepts it "as read").

This brilliantly amusing presentation of the genuine soldier (Bluntschli, the practical Swiss) as opposed to the romantic conception of him (Sergius, the flamboyant "hero") and the true professional nature of war not only won Shaw a modest public at the time—it was his first play to be presented in the commercial theatre—but has kept his popularity green ever since in innumerable productions by companies including famous actors. At the New Theatre in London during the last war there was a notable Old Vic production in which Ralph Richardson played Bluntschli and Laurence Olivier Sergius, and it was as Bluntschli that the brilliant Irish actor, Cyril Cusack, who has staged so many of Shaw's plays in his native Dublin, won the international critics' award of Best Actor of the Festival at the Paris Festival of 1960, sixty-six years after the play's first production.

An explosive objection to the play at the time on the grounds of its supposed insult to the rising nation of Bulgaria, then seeking to shake off a foreign yoke, was wittily parried by Shaw as completely insubstantial and beside the real point of his play, and its entertainment value was such that in 1909 its plot was borrowed without permission for an operetta by the composer Oscar Straus. This was first produced in Berlin and soon afterwards throughout the world under the title *The Chocolate Soldier*, and thus early anticipated *My Fair Lady* by becoming the first Shaw "musical" (in fact Shaw had no hand in it, and in 1927 took action to prevent use of *Arms and the Man* in a film of the musical. Nevertheless, the plot, characters and some dialogue are unmistakably Shavian).

Candida was Shaw's fifth play, although *You Never Can Tell*, a lighter comedy which has continued to hold its own on the stage, preceded it in production by the Stage

Society. Owing to the rich and maternal qualities of its heroine (whom a few perversely find too "managing" for their taste), it is a favorite play with many who profess not to care for Shaw; and the opportunities the chief role provides have across sixty years attracted many famous actresses, from Shaw's friend Janet Achurch (who played it at the Strand in 1900, its first London run) to Dulcie Gray as late as 1960 at Wyndham's Theatre. Shaw in late life vigorously and a little petulantly stormed into print to deny that the character of Candida was based on that of Ellen Terry (who in fact disliked the character). This from the autobiographical point of view is, of course, obviously true; but that Candida, conceived in 1894, did not owe anything, in her feminine warmth and touch of maternal radiance, to Ellen, then Shaw's favorite actress, seems equally obviously unbelievable. Yet we may take it as read that the elderly Shaw was substantially right in that for this character he had no direct model (though he pointed out the name Candida was borrowed from an Italian lady he never met).

"The play," Shaw wrote, "is a counterblast to Ibsen's *Doll's House*, showing that in the real typical doll's house it is the man who is the doll." A few men have not been able to face up to this characteristic of the play, and find insupportable and cruel Candida's revelation at the end that it is, in fact, herself who "wears the trousers" and enables her husband to carry out his manifold duties as a socialistic cleric and lecturer. Like most emotional evaluations it is an unsound one, because it leaves out of consideration the writer's use of "dramatic license" to make his point, which necessitates Morell, as well as the youthful poet Marchbanks, being present. Shaw, though he once wrote with obvious sincerity, "I have certain sensitive places in my soul," had not himself that kind of *amour propre* which becomes bruised at the slightest hint of derogation to his status or masculinity; and it is doubtful if he were capable even of noticing that his scene might, in some eyes, reflect on Candida's natural kindness or actually smack of cruelty. His characters were real enough, as we have noticed, in comparison with the stage women of his day, and his putting of social point before character (if such it is) merely emphasizes that the new license he won for his stage women still did not carry him psychologically as far as a genius like Ibsen.

Yet it is still possible to be oversensitive about Candida here; for her point is not truly derogatory to Morell, her husband, in his work or personal character, but the perfectly true and valid social one, to which any woman who has herself worked out of the home would bear witness today: that for the smooth running of a professional career, giving full time and opportunity for its development, the lifting of the burden of household worries and duties is essential. In this way the woman serves the man and leaves his talent free to expand, even though he may rarely fully grasp the nature of the debt he owes, simply because he is not in a position to grasp the nature of the threat to his work. But any woman with a career will understand Shaw's truth, for it is a basis, too, of woman's general inability, except in outstanding but fairly rare cases, to rival man's output in quantity if not quality of creative work.

One reason (as so often) for the misreading or exaggeration of this dénouement is a long tradition of misplaying in the theatre, and too many Morells on the stage have enforced it by exaggerating the helpless, unctuous or even comic side of the part. But the Reverend James Morell is not a fool or a prig; he is a thoroughly capable, social-minded cleric with a conscience, drawn by a writer who, as he says, "knew practically all the leading Christian Socialist clergymen." His faults are of unobservance and over-dedication to his own work, not of ingrained pomposity or inappreciation of his wife; how else could a woman like Candida have cared for him, and chosen to stick to him in the face of the competition of a younger man with the honey of flattery on his tongue, as well as the exciting incipient genius of a poet?

If Candida, clear-eyed like her name, chose Morell it was because he was lovable and, to her, worthy, and not merely a symbol of male babyhood and dependence; her criticism, gentle but sound, is rather of the poet whose core, as the core of genius must be to survive, is of steel, for all his appeal—which she sees through even more than he does—to her maternal feelings. It is a reason why the 1960 production of *Candida* in London was successful in bringing out the essential humanity of the play; for Mr. Michael Denison as Morell never for one moment suggested a man of straw, unworthy of Candida, but a man seriously, occasionally humorously, and therefore sometimes blindly devoted to his profession, with an implicit basic understanding with his wife which he had never before felt the necessity of analyzing. How much this sensitive interrelationship of Candida and Morell as a normal husband and wife was due to the fact that the actors in this production, Miss Dulcie Gray and Mr. Denison, were themselves married is an interesting question (Janet Achurch and Charles Charrington, who played the parts in the first London production, were also married to each other, but Shaw did not like their performances). The result in the case of Miss Gray and Mr. Denison, both sincere and intelligent players, was illuminating and valuable to the play.

Shaw's deep interest in Shelley as a poet-reformer was lifelong, and it is more than possible Eugene Marchbanks owed something to the volatile younger Shelley, including the vein of steel ignored by his friend and biographer, Jefferson Hogg. Hogg was an egoist whose myth of "ineffectual angel" (with himself as wise guide and corrector) with regard to Shelley Shaw was far too sharp in his understanding of talent and politics not to see through. He later confessed that when conceiving Marchbanks he had in mind De Quincey's account of his adolescence in his *Confessions*. We may take it, therefore, like all stage creations, as a composite portrait drawn both from more than one source in life and from imagination.

Too many stage Marchbanks, too, have fallen into the error of Hogg's "ineffectual angel," giving the character a feminine flaccidity it does not, at base, possess, and which does not at all match up with Candida's final shrewd assessment. Shaw's own shrewdness is discernible in the way in which Candida's estimate reveals the poet's strength for the first time to himself. Critics, looking in Marchbanks for literal signs of poetic genius which Shaw's dialogue does not provide, have often missed Shaw's real success, which is the drawing of a believable and unromanticized *character* of a poet in embryo. Granville Barker, who played the part in the famous Court Theatre production in 1904, had the intellectual iron Shaw probably needed. He had, in fact, immediately envisaged Barker as the right choice for Marchbanks when he first saw him in a Stage Society performance of Hauptmann's *The Coming of Peace* in 1900.

Barker was then twenty-two years old, Shaw forty-four. In Barker he was to find his ideal collaborator as actor, producer and manager, consolidated by the joint venture into management of Barker and the excellent businessman, J. E. Vedrenne, at the Court Theatre in Sloane Square in 1904. More than the Stage Society had done, the Barker-Vedrenne régime at the Court between 1904 and June, 1907, was to mark the real establishment of Shaw as a popular dramatist and vital force in the living theatre. Eleven of his plays (totaling 701 performances) were given there, in addition to other plays by rising dramatists, including Barker himself; and it laid the foundation, too, of Shaw's own close friendship with Barker, who came nearer to the place of son in his affections than any other man. For in him Shaw met not only a person whose charm and talent and looks all, doubtless, appealed to the romantic in him (for there is a romantic lurking behind all who love or write on or for the theatre, and to ignore the vein in Shaw is to lose the key to some of his apparent and mercurial irreconcilabilities); but a theatre worker whose revolutionary drive, efficiency and intellectual capacity in some ways matched his own. The breaking of this friendship in later years, through Barker's self-removal from the theatre under the influence of his rich second wife (who shared the instinctive conformity of American women and hated Shaw), was probably the deepest personal blow Shaw ever suffered, and a sorrow to which he never became completely impervious.

But that was, in 1900, still to come. In the meantime came *The Devil's Disciple*, seized upon by the American actor Richard Mansfield who first presented it in New York in 1897; *Caesar and Cleopatra*, written in 1898 although it also had a foreign *première*, in German under Max Reinhardt at the Neues Theater, Berlin, in March, 1906; and *Captain Brassbound's Conversion*, in which Barker played the part of the American captain, Hamlin Kearney, in the first Stage Society production at the Strand Theatre in December, 1900: thus preserving the link with Shaw, with whom he corresponded on the playing of the role.

The fact that the first-named two plays many years later qualified for filming shows the remarkable tenacity of life Shaw's plays were by now exhibiting. *The Devil's Disciple* is not generally considered a major work; but neither is it in any sense a minor one. It may be said in one way to continue the line of thought on war started in *Arms and the Man* and continued in *Caesar and Cleopatra*; where we reach the zenith of Shaw's approach, the analysis of the character of a military genius, which was to spill over less seriously into the character of Napoleon in *Man of Destiny* and attain the heights again, a quarter of a century later, in *Saint Joan.*

The Devil's Disciple is the meridian of the first trilogy; reflecting a touch of extravaganza from *Arms and the Man* and in the sardonic, witty General Burgoyne (like Caesar, Napoleon and Joan, an historical figure) looking forward to the man chiefly responsible for military victory. Bluntschli is, in essence, the common soldier; Burgoyne the commander; but both prick the bubble of war in their own way just as the Devil's Disciple himself, Dick Dudgeon, does in his. The first two see war from within; Dick, the so-called rapscallion and rebel against society, from without. But in all three the angle is basically witty and sardonic, although in Burgoyne we first see the responsibility of the man who must make the decisions—in his case hamstrung by incompetency from above, a disability making for cynicism which Caesar, the commander *in excelsis,* does not have to endure.

It is this sense of responsibility fettered that makes Burgoyne, apart from his wit, often a more formidable and deeply drawn figure on the stage than the volatile, charming, rebellious Dick, and the part has attracted many fine actors, from Barker at the Savoy (1907) to Esmé Percy, brilliant Shavian actor of the nineteen-thirties, and Sir Laurence Olivier, who played a less concentrated but still potent version of the character in the film. He is the subject, too, of one of Shaw's admirable character sketches in the stage directions of the published play:

> General Burgoyne is 55, and very well preserved. He is a man of fashion, gallant enough to have made a distinguished marriage by an elopement, witty enough to write successful comedies, aristocratically connected enough to have had opportunities of high military distinction. His eyes, large, brilliant, apprehensive and intelligent, are his most remarkable feature. . . .

And as if this were not enough he has, too, one of the most likable of Shaw's wittier comments on stage reactions (following a remark of Dick's in the prisoner's dock, "I never expect a soldier to think"):

> Burgoyne is boundlessly delighted at this retort, which almost reconciles him to the loss of America.

Dick Dudgeon, nevertheless, is far from the puppet romantic hero of the "melodrama" formula on which Shaw—with his ironic habit of turning his dramatic coats inside out—based his play. He represents what Shaw in his Preface calls "the Diabolonian position" in the play: "With all his mother's indomitable selffulness, but with Pity instead of Hatred as his master passion, he pities the devil; takes his side; and champions him, like a true Covenanter, against the world. He thus becomes, like all genuinely religious men, a reprobate and an outcast."

The harsh puritanism of Mrs. Dudgeon gives the opening of the play its will-reading scene, a scene of ironic satire of human hypocrisy as old as Ben Jonson's *Volpone* and as new as Puccini's opera *Gianni Schicci*; it is a preparation only for the rebellion against society and its wars to come. First and foremost, *The Devil's Disciple* is a "morality" play. But the basis of romantic melodrama remains, and it is not by chance Dick has appealed to romantic actors like Mansfield, Sir John Martin-Harvey and Robert Donat.

As I wrote in another book[1]: "The appeal of the play to Harvey was obvious. Dick Dudgeon, with a Shavian twist, is in all externals the hero of romantic melodrama made popular by Harvey in such plays as *The Breed of the Treshams*. Here are the same scapegrace charm, the same suggestion of a heart of gold beneath the reprobate's banter, the same heroic self-sacrifice; and the plot contains even the bland melodramatic trick of the last-minute res-

[1] *Old Vic Drama,* Rockliff, London, 1948.

cue from the scaffold. Yet it is just that Shavian twist that gives the whole character and play their new spirit and ironic fun. It is melodrama brought without sentimentality into the cool light of reason, and transformed by a wit not the less dazzling for its underlying irony. As a result the play has twice the intellectual seriousness of the average melodrama as well as twice its fun; and it survives to-day on that basis of humour and truth, while the romantic melodramas of the Harvey school have been whistled away by the wind."

It is worth noting briefly, in the character of Anderson, the parson who has missed his true vocation as a soldier, a first representative of an idea of Shaw's about the militant cleric which he repeated years later in the character of Ferrovius in *Androcles and the Lion.* The thread of most of Shaw's main arguments and lines of thought can be traced throughout his works; he was never above using a good idea or character twice, and his intellectual consistency was remarkable considering his long career.

So *The Devil's Disciple* leads quite naturally to *Caesar and Cleopatra,* Shaw's first major study of the great man in his achievement and isolation. "I have found flocks and pastures, men and cities, but no other Caesar" says his Julius Caesar; just as the loneliness of the saint is overcome in his Joan of Arc's great cry: "What is my loneliness, compared with the loneliness of God?" But as a study of the qualities that set genius apart from the rest of mankind, its emphasis is not only on the apartness in what might be called social terms, but on other attributes most relevant to a great general and commander of men, including the quality of courage.

Wagner's boy Siegfried, also, is a study in fearlessness, and if Ibsen influenced Shaw in some directions it is inescapable that his other god as a critic, Wagner, influenced him equally at times in the matter of philosophy and dramatic ideas. The boy Siegfried, intended saviour of mankind because without fear and its corruptive force, is different from Shaw's Caesar because the fearlessness has different springs—*i.e.* innocence of life and total lack of imagination in the matter of death or danger. Caesar's fearlessness is certainly not through either; he is what Siegfried might have become had he developed in *Götterdämmerung* into a hero of mature thought as well as action, and not died in his prime owing to a mechanism of plot into which Wagner, for once defeated by his saga material and his own dramatic impulses, became too involved to disentangle himself.

Wagner got himself out of the difficulty and recovered his own genius by reasserting himself as a musician and composing for his dead victim a funeral march fit not only for a hero but for a god: thus creating a tragic splendor that musically, if not dramatically, makes *Götterdämmerung* appear almost a *King Lear* of the operatic stage. But Wagner's models were Shakespeare and the Greeks, and Shaw was no Shakespearean romantic. His Caesar was a revolt against Shakespeare's denigration of the great general in order, as he saw it, to romanticize "the Nonconformist Conscience which he personified as Brutus." He is a mature man of fifty-four, long enough in control of the reins of power to understand all the corrupt motivations of those wishing to seize them from him, and wise and cool enough in judgment to know that the best way to retain command in a tricky business is to recognize that "He who has never hoped can never despair" and—as Shaw's Don Juan in the third Act of *Man and Superman* later put it—"It is not death that matters, but the fear of death."

Shaw maintained that his Caesar was true to history in a way Shakespeare's was not, and in this he was certainly right. This does not mean to say that his creative imagination does not illuminate and change the portrait, and invest it with a quality of vision, wit and commentary that were essentially Shaw's own. Caesar is not just Caesar —Plutarch's, Mommsen's or the self-portrait as far as it emerges in *De Bello Gallico*—he is also Shaw's own version of the superman which sprang from his lifelong realization—in spite of his theoretic socialism—that men were not equal mentally and in abilities of statesmanship, and that it is suicidal for democracy to attempt government on the fallacy that they are.

In later life, it was to mislead him (though not as much as his enemies' misinterpretations would make it appear) into acceptance of some of the principles of Hitler's regime in Germany and of Stalin's in Soviet Russia. And in *theory* he was by no means always wrong—except in the basic and appalling mistake of assuming that either leader might be truly as fine and noble-minded a dictator as his own Caesar, and therefore a fit politician to put the theories into practice. Shaw's inability as a dramatist to create a true villain was echoed in this kind of fallacy in his political thinking: surprisingly for a wit and ironist of his nature, he hated injustice and cruelties of government and indeed anything not designed for the human good, yet had no hatred in his heart for individual men and women, though he sometimes saw through them penetratingly enough. His own personal kindness strangely at times limited his vision of others' motives; but also he refused to condemn blindly or wholeheartedly where he saw certain good to society, and in this at least remained throughout his life a valuable balancer in heated controversies. Such are necessary in all ages; and no one who knew anything of Shaw's private life or really studied his works could assume for a moment that, even if he made mistakes of judgment, they were the result of anything but a complete and disinterested desire for social and human good.

What marks his Caesar is also a fine prose and quality of thought in the man's own speeches—great rhythmic prose threnodies and a gift to the actor of substance. The part was written for Forbes-Robertson, Shaw's ideal as a classical actor, and a later great actor, Sir Laurence Olivier, has also been superlatively successful in it. With Cleopatra he is less successful by ideal standards, though successful enough along his own lines in creating a witty, youthful image of kittenish seductiveness, hardening under Caesar's own teaching into something altogether more ruthless and cruel, a herald of future power wielded out of egoism, not for the common good. Basically, his Cleopatra is a designing minx as unerotic as Caesar, in spite of her hopeful image of the strong arms of a returning Mark Antony. Shaw, the natural puritan, made no bones about his despisal of the Shakespearean conception of Antony as a tragic figure, ruined by passion; such eroticism, he asserted with force, was not a matter of tragedy but ludicrous debasement, and in his own plays he would have none of it.

Curiously enough, it never affected his judgment of *Tristan und Isolde* in the same way, as we have seen, partly owing to the transforming power of the music. And he could write, too, percipiently enough of Parsifal: ". . . that long kiss of Kundry's from which he learns so much is one of those pregnant simplicities which stare the world in the face for centuries, and yet are never pointed out except by great men." But Wagner, of course, working in the different field of music-drama, did not challenge Shaw's crusading zeal for the conception of a new social-minded drama as Shakespeare did. When he liked, Shaw could write of Shakespeare, too, admiringly and percipiently enough, confessing freely in later life that his campaign against his works had been a necessary critical attack on public taste to make way for the new-style genius of Ibsen, not to count his own revolutionary methods as a dramatist. His analysis and demolition of the distortions of the true Shakespeare by the Victorian actor-managers show this to be true, and his understanding of Shakespeare greater than that of some who superficially pass judgment on Shaw as a denigrator of his plays. Shaw's life, as we have seen, was not without its own occasional emotional associations and problems, which were to come to a head some years after he wrote *Caesar and Cleopatra* in the tempestuous (for him) friendship with Mrs. Patrick Campbell—for whom, in fact, he actually wrote the part of Cleopatra, though she did not see eye to eye enough with Forbes-Robertson (or he with her) to play it in any major production. Her company gave it its first "copyright" performance, still customary in those times, at Newcastle in 1899; but further productions in England were long delayed and without her, Forbes-Robertson himself first playing it in New York in 1906.

Caesar apart, the play holds the stage thoroughly entertainingly but without achieving the cohesion or purpose of true greatness. It degenerates into a frolic in which Ftatateeta and her unfortunate name (in spite of her basically strong characterization) become a tiresomely repetitive joke, although Britannus, Shaw's characteristic tilt at the conservative and moral Englishman out of his time, creates more joy still for the audience than some of his sourer critics will allow (in these times of altered moral standards in England he has, though, become finally out-of-date as satire, although the comic portrait, being based on living memory, has still not lost its complete success as a national joke). Rufio remains an excellent characterization of rough outspoken soldierly loyalty, and Apollodorus in the right hands can be a figure of dashing rapscallion fun and charm, as Robert Helpmann in the Olivier production of 1951 engagingly showed.

Captain Brassbound's Conversion is the least successful of the three plays, and Shaw himself in a letter to Granville-Barker showed he had occasional misgivings and felt it needed some rewriting. Brassbound himself, the "black sheep" smuggler of good family half-tamed by the warmly maternal English lady, Lady Cecily, owed something doubtless to that romantic Elizabethan-out-of-his-time, the traveler, gaucho, socialist politician and fine prose writer, R. B. Cunninghame Graham, whose adventurous attempt to penetrate what Shaw calls "the inviolate recesses of Morocco" was lifted by Shaw on his own admission into his play.

The main importance of the play biographically is that the character of Lady Cecily was written for Ellen Terry, who appeared in the part with Laurence Irving in his father's company at Liverpool for the "copyright" performance in October, 1899, and again at the Court Theatre under the Barker management on March 20, 1906, for a series of six matinees. Ellen had wounded Shaw greatly by her dislike of the play, until she actually played in it, when she changed her mind. It was the occasion—at the Royal Court—of their first serious meetings, and of her romance with James Carew whom she shortly afterwards married, as I (or rather Shaw) described in an earlier chapter.

The part was glove-fitted to her special qualities of warm personal radiance and humane serene ability to handle and enchant the roughest diamonds among men, and the basic truth of the character and situation has been vouched for by a later actress of it, Dame Flora Robson, who described to me with enjoyment how, inspired by her own revival of the play, she herself took a holiday in Marrakesh, where an Arab chieftain greeted with uproarious enchantment and delight her polite echoing of Lady Cecily's "How d'you do?," with outstretched gloved hand, on meeting him. From that moment onwards, she says, she was treated throughout her stay "like the Queen of Morocco."

But Dame Flora had, for five years in early life, given up acting to supervise the workers in a factory, and found that friendly relations with its heavy laborers, as unsophisticated as the Arabs of Morocco, came easily to her, and she had them soon in the palm of her hand. Here again, therefore, we find a Lady Cecily naturally in tune with Shaw's characterization, emphasizing its truth to human nature. When writing to ask his permission to do the play she explained this, but also admitted that although she felt she thoroughly understood the part she was worried because she felt she was not beautiful, as it seemed to require. Shaw's characteristic and kindly response to this was a comparison of her with a French actress—the beauty, he said, does not matter, for it was "inside" her as an actress. He also referred with admiration, graphically enough, to what he described as her "gin-soaked voice": a quality likewise belonging to the French actress, and accepted by Dame Flora with some amusement.

He allowed her to tour the play, but in this late period of life his strange obsession—a fabulously rich old man—that State taxation was ruining him caused him to forbid her to bring it into the West End of London, where it might have earned him large sums in royalties which would (he was convinced) double his taxation rate.

His heroines, suggests this fine and emotional actress, are habitually "cold"; for this reason "warm" actresses are required for them. It is an interesting theory, technically sound in the theatre. In the same way, an over-emotional actor in training needs a certain concentration on unemotional parts, and *vice versa*, just as any front-rank teacher of dancing knows that the naturally classical, lyrical student dancer needs the discipline of the harder forms of technique, including *batterie* (or beats in footwork, never easy for the poetic ballerina) and stronger steps generally.

Chapter 7

Success and the Court Theatre

COUNTING AN UNIMPORTANT stage version (in blank verse) of his novel, *Cashel Byron's Profession*, under the title *The Admirable Bashville*, as eleventh, Shaw's twelfth play was his first genuine triumph: so much so that its title, *Man and Superman*, has dropped more or less into the English language and become almost synonymous with the name Bernard Shaw, as well as popularly most associated with his philosophy.

Although finished and "copyrighted" in the usual way in 1903, and given token performances by the Stage Society at the Royal Court in 1905, its first public performances were by the Vedrenne-Barker management at the Royal Court Theatre, with the same cast, beginning on May 23, 1905, and its 176 performances were the greatest number achieved there by a Shaw play under this regime.

It should be explained that the Royal Court performances were of the shortened version of the play normally performed in theatres, and omitted Act III, which was later presented at the Court under the title *Don Juan in Hell* in 1907, for eight matinees. The immense length of the full play has made this practice inevitable, as from the purely constructional point of view the Don Juan episode is an irrelevant interlude in which the characters assume the roles of the leading figures of Mozart's opera, *Don Giovanni*, supposedly their ancestors. Yet intellectually it is, as Shaw himself fully realized, the core of the play, which without it becomes an entertaining comedy of the pursuit of the male by the female for purposes of marriage and reproduction of the species; whereas with it

Shaw's basic philosophy falls into place through his expanding of his theory of the Life Force as the motivating energy behind human relationships and the unconscious battle for human survival, with intellectual man's rebellion against it and all the purely sensual pleasures of Hell.

It is not, of course, his own invention in this sense, being only an extension of Schopenhauer's idea of Will as (in the words of Thomas Mann) "the ultimate, irreducible, primeval principle of being . . . the impelling force producing the whole visible world and all life—for it is the will to live." Its opposite, the Death-Wish, had already been imperishably enshrined in music by Wagner, partly under Schopenhauer influence, in *Tristan und Isolde*. Perhaps this is why Shaw chose to illuminate the more vital philosophy theatrically through another musical analogy, Mozart's *Don Giovanni*; for the legend of Don Juan appropriately enough is a legend based, by modern psychological standards, on the urge for life and procreation, not unmixed with an eroticism which is really the nervous energy to "prove" a virility suspected to be lacking.

With this side of the matter, needless to say, Shaw is not deeply concerned, beyond making his Juan satiated and cynical in a Hell in which Donna Anna has become a mere nuisance of a single, undeveloped purpose. It is the Will to Live, and Cult of the Superman (an extension yet again of Wagner's Siegfried, created to release Man from the tainted rule of the Gods) that become Shaw's driving force behind the play: the "wheel within wheels" that gives direction, profundity and purpose to the surface comedy of sexual relationships.

"Modern theology," wrote Shaw in the note to the Court Theatre program, "conceives heaven and hell, not as places, but as states of the soul; and by the soul it means, not an organ like the liver, but the divine element common to all life, which causes us 'to do the Will of God' in addition to looking after our individual interests, and to honor one another solely for our divine activities and not at all for our selfish activities." His Don Juan, in this setting of a Hell only of the soul's damnation, ruled by a gentlemanly Devil boldly expostulating his theory of Hell's pleasure as "the true law of life," becomes a man banished to it by the ghost of the Commandant he had killed and whose "statue" he had in a famous scene invited sardonically to supper. But this Hell of earthly pleasures is a Hell indeed —no Paradise in reverse as the Devil blandly suggests— for Don Juan, now (again in Shaw's words) "consumed with a passion for divine contemplation and creative activity, this being the secret of the failure of love to interest him permanently. In his imagination is a finer form of life, of creative contemplation and pure thought, made possible by human development of the Superman above earthly greed and passion."

The argument—Shaw was to return to some of it again in the final scene of *Back to Methuselah*—is no flat statement but vitalized by a lively discussion in which the Devil has a no less insinuating case for a contrary rule of life, as well as one of the longest speeches and tests of actors' memory in the history of the stage. Its fine muscular prose, echoed at almost equal length by Juan himself, shows at its most brilliant Shaw's ability to keep any thought or philosophy out of the narrowing limitations of the unarguable (a fault of many inferior dramatists of our time), and to allow the opposite side its strongest and apparently most valid arguments. "Beware the pursuit of the Superman: it leads to an indiscriminate contempt for the Human" declares the Devil; and history since this play was written has chillingly shown he spoke with greater truth, in words commanding greater respect, than Shaw himself even realized.

This long and brilliant but seldom played interlude apart (Esmé Percy, Alec Clunes and John Clements are courageous actor-managers who have staged it in London from the thirties onwards), *Man and Superman* retains its popularity as a comedy embodying humanity's favorite theme for entertainment, the making of marriages by female will against the natural masculine instinct to escape the chains of a single, responsible relationship. As such, it is—recalling Shakespeare's Buckingham—less deep-revolving than witty: kept alive by the amusing, ineffectual but at least valiantly fought battle of the highly intelligent man, John Tanner, to resist the wiles of a young woman whose sole interest in him (it would appear) is sexual and procreative, but who musters her forces with an unswerving and meticulously planned strategy worthy of a general on the field of war. Tanner in one sense is Shaw himself (Barker in the Court production made up like him, with a beard), author of *The Revolutionist's Handbook and Pocket Companion*, and at least gifted with an Irish flood of words that put up a sparkling battery of ack-ack fire against attack. If they prove unavailing in the end, he is an opponent at least worthy as relentless a tactician as Ann, a fact she recognizes (in a not unpenetrating flash of psychological insight by Shaw) when she genuinely collapses, with a release of overcharged tension, in relief and almost disbelief at her final victory.

In other ways Ann, for all the charm any actress can give her, is not an attractive creation, and close to satire in Shaw's use of her uncomprisingly as a symbol of Victorian hypocrisy and a representative of feminine ruthlessness in sexual pursuit. If she showed the slightest interest in Tanner mentally, or appreciation of his work and its cost to him (for all work of his kind is costly in energy and mental peace), we might warm to her more; but actually Shaw is psychologically not unshrewd here, for frequently enough this is the kind of woman men of intelligence are basically attracted by, yield to, marry, and in a remarkable number of cases remain faithful to, even though they may sometimes secretly regret some deeper lack in the relationship. It is, of course, sex triumphant, a fact of life Shaw, despite his instinctive revulsion, was honest enough to recognize as overriding in action.

His stage direction description of Ann is, as always, revealing, and explains much if the actress (as does not always happen, for the part invites coquetry) can interpret it: "Turn up her nose, give a cast to her eye, replace her black and violet confection by the apron and feathers of the flower girl, strike all the aitches out of her speech, and Ann would still make men dream.[1] Vitality is as common as humanity; but, like humanity, it sometimes rises to genius; and Ann is one of the vital geniuses."

Most of the attacks on this play by outraged feminists (mainly male romantics) spring from an assumption that in Ann Whitefield Shaw was presenting his own first and last word on women. In fact he was, of course, pinpointing one particular type, in order to emphasize one particular allegory—that of the Life Force which is not only the source of man's intellectual achievements but of generation and his perpetuity in time: the one threatening to destroy the other, and therefore perpetually at war. Nowadays we call it the sex war. In this force which resides mainly in women—many, but not all, women—the man though attractive and often carefully selected is mainly the instrument of this force of nature, the maternal instinct which is the instinct to create children. Frustrated, it can wreak great havoc, not the least at times by concentrating its maternal possessiveness and domination on the man. In exceptional cases, where a child is born, the child itself becomes the object of the stifling, single-purpose affection and reaps the resultant havoc in the form either of an

[1] The faint looking-forward here to Eliza Doolittle is interesting, and shows how Shaw's mind works ahead in ideas only fully used later.

Oedipus complex[2] or homosexuality or impotence with women (not the same thing, though often confused in the mind of a cynical, oversophisticated society, for whom a little Freud is definitely a dangerous thing). Either way, the husband suffers.

Ann herself gives certain signs of becoming such a woman, had she not possessed the controlling brakes of the will power and personal magic to make her man both marry and desire her, thus fulfilling the ultimate need of her nature as an instrument of the Life Force. Thereafter, Jack Tanner can be expected to take care of himself: he has other fish to fry, of greater importance in his own mind and no less creative. It may not be a happy marriage; but it may work to the reasonable contentment of both parties. The world is full of such. It is where the man himself has a genuinely romantic attachment, and dependence on its fulfillment apart from his own work, that real unhappiness is likely to ensue.

This would have been the marriage of Ann and the devoted Tavy, as Shaw and probaby Ann herself both knew. And his remark regarding Tavy that a broken heart can be a not unpleasant thing in London on £2,000 a year is more penetrating and compassionate, and less cynical, than many might assume: for Shaw had known the stings of poverty without love. We have no reason to suppose—and indeed it is very unlikely from his later history with women—that Shaw's chastity until the age of twenty-nine was entirely his own choice, or without its unhappy frustrations. He himself wrote frankly that no woman would look at him before that age because of his poverty and the miserable appearance he presented: he had, on the surface, nothing to offer a woman. Although he is under-

[2] The Freudian expression is an unfortunate misnomer in some ways, for Oedipus' marriage with Jocasta was probably one made originally for reasons of state. We certainly have no evidence to the contrary in Sophocles' play, as Freud himself realized.

standably reticent on the subject ("I have certain sensitive places in my soul," he once wrote as we have seen) his phrasing suggests that he had put the matter to the test and been rejected; and such rejections in youth can not only hurt deeply (even if the wound is one partly of *amour propre)* but linger painfully and create psychological complexes for many years to come, as anyone who has heard a sensitive man talk of such an early experience—however lightly—cannot fail to realize.

That Shaw never mentioned his experiences prior to his first successful one, with Mrs. Jenny Paterson, only makes the assumption of his earlier wounds more likely. It explains, too, his inability to break with her, in spite of her scenes and possessiveness, for so long: the feeling was almost certainly one of gratitude in addition to a response, deepened by long abstinence, to her passionate nature. If afterwards he talked and wrote about the experience too much—his chivalry to women in private life was otherwise marked, which makes this the more notable—it is hard to evade the conclusion that this was a natural and not unpathetic masculine pride at this first improbable demonstration of his virility and power to attract women, instead of repel them. Under it, his own sex appeal and charm of personality flowered, as happens with a woman in similar circumstances; so much so—though helped, of course, by his subsequent fame which attracts a certain type of person on its own account—that in the end it far outpaced his own rarer ability to respond, and he was able to say with obvious truth that where women were concerned he was infinitely more hunted than hunter.

Quite apart from the more passionate Julia Craven and others of Shaw's creation owing much to Mrs. Paterson, ranging to Joan of Arc at the other end of the scale, it is obvious that Ann Whitefield cannot be taken by any reasonable being as an attack by Shaw on women as a whole. His own far wider experience with intellectual women and social workers, including Annie Besant, Beatrice Webb, Charlotte his wife and innumerable others, must demolish this nonsense at once—though Beatrice Webb's openly passionate "babying" of Sidney, which often irritated Shaw, did not pass unnoticed either, and Shaw was hardly likely to make the mistake of assuming, as many men do, that the "new woman" released into society when Ibsen's Nora Helmer slammed the door in her husband's face was of necessity a woman who had lost all her primeval instincts or capacity to love, possessive or otherwise.

If an actress like Dame Flora Robson finds Shaw's heroines cold and in need of histrionic warming, it is in many cases only a surface truth, meaning only that Shaw's interest in women was less emotional than intellectually sympathetic. To the end he maintained, in play, prose and private life, that the Life Force in its sexual aspect disrupted more important aspirations of human life and society; that women had been the victim of man's own sense of superiority in these things too long; and that they had a wider part to play in the world than the making of a home and bearing of children. The domestic instinct (at least as a full-time occupation) is no more an essential part of being a woman than a gift for "do-it-yourself" and electrical engineering is to be taken for granted as an essential part of the business of being a man. In his appreciation of this Shaw was widening the frontiers not only of women in real life but of women as characters on the stage. With him, the Victorian conventional picture of women, good and bad, as victims solely of domesticity or sexual passion (hypocritically obscured though this may have been) vanished for ever from the theatre: with the result that an altogether wider range of subjects as dramatic material became available to writers for the stage.

Man and Superman was a last shot at the stage woman for whom the attraction of a mate was the whole purpose of life; and the play is a classic because its subject and the Life Force in this aspect remain a driving and sometimes destructive power in human society which the birth of the "new woman" can never fully overcome, as Shaw well knew. Ann Whitefield stands for all eternity until the race shall end; but she is no longer the only pebble on the feminine beach, and this her creator also knew. She was represented for the first time without Victorian hypocrisy. After her, as after Julia Craven, anything became possible, from *A Streetcar Named Desire* to *A Taste of Honey*: developments her creator may well have viewed with surprise and misgiving, as often happens to the revolutionaries who open up new paths for society to tread.

The fact remains that John Murray, the publisher, turned down *Man and Superman* for publication on grounds of its disgraceful immorality as a picture of women. Audiences have never had the same fastidious inhibitions, and the play, as we have seen, was the greatest success in the short but distinguished and historically important life of the Royal Court Theatre under the Barker management.

In number of performances *You Never Can Tell* and *John Bull's Other Island* came next in order of popularity, and though neither merits nor has received anything like the same fame or number of revivals, both have held their own down the years and never quite vanished from the stage.

"If *Candida* is one of the best of Mr. Shaw's plays for the completeness with which it contains and finishes its story, *John Bull's Other Island*," wrote Desmond McCarthy of the original Court Theatre production, "is remarkable for being equally successful for entirely different reasons. It is a play with hardly any story, with no climax, without the vestige of a plot, and without anything like an ending; in fact without one of the qualities of the 'well-constructed' play; yet it is nevertheless an absolute success."

In this he showed exceptional enlightenment for the critic

not merely of his own day but for forty years afterwards; for it is only in the last decade in England that critics have learned to accept without vilification any play not written according to rule (meaning by "rule" nineteenth-century "rule," for it never applied to the Elizabethans and Jacobeans), and their conversion is so recent that Bertolt Brecht himself is still suspect, in spite of the imitations of his English followers. (The fact that this revolution in English theatrical taste came from the Royal Court Theatre of the fifties is a touch that would have pleased Shaw. "Every dream is a prophecy; every jest is an earnest in the womb of Time," as the unfrocked priest Keegan says finely in his play.)

It is possible, nevertheless, that McCarthy overestimated. The success of *John Bull's Other Island* is not absolute, though certainly relative. Candida, Morell and Marchbanks all have some grasp on our imagination and personal feeling: they interest us enough as people for us to care about their future. I doubt if Larry Doyle, the hard-headed, antiidealist Irishman in rebellion against his country's suspect romanticism, or Tom Broadbent, the English sentimentalist who does not let his sentimentality interfere with a good business deal, interest us greatly as human beings; they are clever representatives of Shaw's cool-headed and devastating assessment of an Ireland that exists only in the imagination of Englishmen, deliberately fed by the Irish themselves. Nora, faithful to Larry yet too quickly won by his friend, is not the strongest of Shaw's feminine characterizations, though like most of his women she has an element of truth new to the theatre of his time. And we are unlikely to remember the rest, and recognize or speak of them by name, as we remember or recognize O'Casey's Paycock or Joxer Daly or Covey or Nora Clitheroe.

But *John Bull's Other Island* is still the work of a genius, and that genius is in the character and words of Keegan, the "mad" priest who is first discovered on the hillside of Rosscullen conversing with a grasshopper—a fancy which points Shaw himself very much as an Irishman, for it is one which no English dramatist, unless writing for children, would think of using, more especially in connection with a character who, so far from being mad, gives every indication throughout of being the sanest person and deepest thinker on the stage. From him stems all this play's mature wisdom and deep-cutting irony, gently expressed yet devastating in impact; and in him is a good deal of Shaw himself with his humane and compassionate regard for animals, the meanest creature of the field—the regard that kept him a rigid vegetarian and anti-vivisectionist throughout his life—as well as his clarity of vision into the meaningless humbug of big business "amelioration" of human conditions, and its tightening grip on the future. Written in 1904, the play is a remarkable indictment of a world we live in still more inescapably today: "For four wicked centuries the world has dreamed this foolish dream of efficiency, and the end is not yet. But the end will come."

That end we have not seen yet, but with the development of the hydrogen bomb may well do so in our time. And for all who travel the world's cities with open eyes, from London and New York in the West to Tokyo in the East, there is the same impression of a civilization feverishly rocketing itself, in a burst of neon lights, commercialism and neurotic insecurity, to a destruction no less complete than the destruction of Rome and Babylon in other ages. There comes a moment when material wealth of the few at the expense of the many (and it is still in that world ratio outside our capital cities today) embitters and deadens the minds of even those who hold it. Shaw knew this; Keenan knew it; and the result was a play in which we are conscious, in the ex-priest, of a new conception of Hell, a Hell here on earth built of our own hands and to our own secret despair.

In the end, this is a mystic play, and its modern version of the Holy Trinity is declaimed by Keenan, in answer to a question as to what heaven is like in his dreams:

> In my dreams it is a country where the State is the Church and the Church the people: three in one and one in three. It is a commonwealth in which work is play and play is life: three in one and one in three. It is a temple in which the priest is the worshipper and the worshipper the worshipped: three in one and one in three. It is a godhead in which all life is human and all humanity divine: three in one and one in three. It is, in short, the dream of a madman.

Not orthodox religion, certainly; but a religion that Dr. Albert Schweitzer would understand. Not orthodox poetry, either; but poetry that Shelley and Byron and De Lorca, the poet-rebels against conformity, would recognize; just as Sybil Thorndike, creator of Shaw's Saint Joan in England and great actress of Shakespeare and Greek tragedy, recognized it in Joan's speech on the loneliness of the saint in Rouen Cathedral, where others of a less-trained and more faulty musical "ear" have denied it. (Dame Sybil, like Shaw himself, was trained in music; and musicians can trace the echo, however remote, of the lyre of Apollo.)

John Bull was the first play of Shaw's to be produced on the stage before its written publication. Its success with the public was great and King Edward VII saw and enjoyed it, thus adding to its favorable publicity and putting Shaw at last firmly on the map as a dramatist.

Major Barbara, written in 1905 and presented at the Court Theatre for six matinees the same year, seems to have sprung in one sense from Keenan's speeches in *John Bull's Other Island*. Shaw's thought worked in a continuous spiral, one play seeming to sow the seed of idea from which the next developed; and it may well be that Keenan's great indictment of capitalism needed, in Shaw's deeper consciousness, the further exploration of the theme of poverty, and its relationship to religion, which is the core of his "Salvation Army" play, *Major Barbara.* (One ignores in this case the interlude of the 1904 one-acter, *How He Lied to Her Husband,* written like so many of Shaw's curtain-raisers in the Court and later periods in response to the need of an actress or manager friend. His major plays are the ones that reflect seriously his development of ideas and processes of thought: social, moral and philosophic. The others remain in most cases entertaining *pièces de theâtre,* outside the scope of a biography of this length. Shaw would certainly have thought so.)

He called the play frankly "A Discussion in Three Acts," with particular truth in Act III, set at Undershaft's factory of armaments, where the crisis of Barbara's passionate spiritual urge to help humanity, and her father's to achieve wealth (and some incidental benefits to his workers) by manufacturing instruments for its ultimate destruction, comes to a head. The hardheaded practical idealist in Shaw did not shirk the outcome: Barbara's own realization that the helping of the poor through religious channels only scrapes the surface of the problem, and there is better work for her here in her father's factory community, in which there is every material consideration and no spiritual fulfillment. But the decision is not arrived at without bitterness, any more than Barbara's decision to leave the Salvation Army rather than to join them in accepting the bribe of the manufacturer of the whiskey which destroys their battle to revive human dignity.

What matters theatrically is that this third act of *Major Barbara*—like that other long "discussion" scene between Warwick, Cauchon and de Stogumber in *Saint Joan*—has such argumentative force and wit that it habitually holds its audience's rapt attention and therefore entertains it, in the best sense of the word, no less completely than if the dramatist were indulging in popular melodramatics. This, perhaps, has been Shaw's greatest gift to the theatre of our time. To make an audience listen, think, and actually *enjoy* listening and thinking, was no mean feat after four hundred years of stage concentration on conventions far removed from thought or the real business of daily life. The gap between the literary worlds of the novel and the theatre has never been so wide since.

The rest of the play is more than entertaining, and the scene in the Salvation Army shelter in the East End of London, with its echoing war cries of "Blood and Fire" mingled with the beating of Cusins' drum and the wavering resistance of Bill Walker's conscience, takes the stage like an Army banner and was no less successful in a film version. Here Shaw, who knew his background well from his social and Borough Council work, created character with a rarer richness than is apparent in many of his plays set in wealthier households, and old "Rummy" Mitchens, Peter Shirley (the workman "too old at forty-six," not completely unknown today), "Snobby" Price (good enough to be brilliantly played by a "star" actor, Emlyn Williams, in the film) and the obstreperous Bill Walker himself echo in some ways the Dickensian note that seeps into this Shaw play about the rapscallion, as well as worthy, poor.

Cusins, the Professor of Greek, was founded on Shaw's old friend Professor Gilbert Murray, famous for his Swinburnian translations of Greek tragedy, and both he and Andrew Undershaft, the armaments manufacturer, need fine actors, and have been played by many "stars," from Granville-Barker (the original) to Maurice Evans and Rex Harrison in the first case and from Louis Calvert to Cecil Trouncer and Robert Morley in the second. As for Barbara, her creator, Annie Russell, at the Court was replaced at a number of performances by Lillah McCarthy, one of the most famous actresses of her day and Granville-Barker's first wife; and later portrayers of the role have included Sybil Thorndike, Wendy Hiller and Moira Shearer.

In one sense, politically, *Major Barbara* never "dates." I remember during its revival at the Old Vic in 1935 how apt and vivid its final act in the munition factory became under the impact of the Japanese invasion of Manchuria; and to the world's sorrow there has been no occasion since when a revival would not reflect a vital current of world argument on some diplomatic or invasion crisis. It is a common criticism of the play of ideas that it vanishes in the dust of the controversy with which it concerned itself, and which inevitably has "settled" with time. But this is only true where the play is in the first case superficial, and concerned with only one issue. A mind like Shaw's has an historical perspective and knows that human history is continually repeating itself; the deeper challenges are never resolved, and echo through time like the murder of Agamemnon, the returning warrior, by the wife who has been faithless to him while he fought at the Siege of Troy (or the Battle of Hastings, or at Gettysburg, or in Flanders, or at Pearl Harbor, or what have you). The patterns of human behavior and social and political expediency are mutable only in degree; a Socrates does not become outmoded because Greek civilization has changed to American or Russian, nor a Shaw or Ibsen because we have new sanitary laws and have in part conquered certain diseases. And when Clytemnestra in the *Agamemnon* coolly invites her husband's mistress-slave into her house with the proud claim that here she need not fear ill-treatment, for this is a house of the old aristocracy, not of the "new rich" created by the war, who do not know how to treat servants with consideration—then and in moments like them two thousand years slip away unnoticed, and we are back with human beings and their problems of society and character as they have existed through every revolution and war and under every system of government.

Certainly Shaw's *Doctor's Dilemma*, the last of his major plays produced at the Court Theatre, has proved as undated as Molière's *Le Malade Imaginaire*, and like *Pygmalion* and *Major Barbara* has been the subject of a popular film. Shaw described it under the title as "A Tragedy," but here we sense his ironic quip at the tragedy of medical incompetence or its professional myths, and not any conviction that the death of the artist Dubedat from their ministrations might so color the whole nature of the play. William Archer, however, had complained that Shaw had never written a "tragedy"—meaning a play ending in a death—and Shaw's description was double-barbed.

It is, of course, an extravagant comedy by Shaw at his most sparkling—"extravagant" in the sense that it is, even more than *Arms and the Man*, an "extravaganza" by nature, a burlesque at least in the case of "B.B." among the doctors in performance. Scene after scene in this sense might be cartooned successfully in *Punch* or *The New Yorker*, with readers' reactions no different from those of theatre audiences, who have roared their way through this play in paroxysms of laughter in many successive revivals. As an indictment of the medical profession it is not serious; but it wields a surgeon's knife of cutting edge. Shaw's hatred of vivisection and all such scientific methods of "benefiting" mankind made him on principle an inexorable opposer of a great deal of medical assumptions and jargon, and it is unfortunate for doctors that his own triumphant longevity almost devoid of their ministrations, and on a diet which by any standards would be considered abstemious, has given him an advantage of the field in the long run.

In fact, as usual, though riotously exaggerating in the cause of comedy, Shaw was basically serious and highly knowledgeable in his background; he was the lifelong friend of many doctors, and a student of Darwin, Lamarck and others working along lines of Evolution and Natural Selection (this was to come to fruition too in *Back to Methuselah*). "Half-witted monomaniacs" was his description of Lister and Pavlov, whose experiments in the cause of science to Shaw's mind in fact never materially furthered science while causing needless suffering in its name; and his description of himself as an "anti-biologist" sprang from this inherent hatred of what was to him (and there is some support for him) a crucifixion of animal life on the erroneous ground that it can prolong the human—in any case, on Shaw's reckoning, by no means always as worth prolonging, morally, as that of the animal.

He knew well enough, too, the shams of the "bedside manner" and the type of doctor fattening on society and the idle hypochondria of fashionable women—no less than the privations and self-sacrifice of the general practitioner in the slum area, such as Dr. Blenkinsop in this play: as he wrote in his Preface, they were common table-talk among the doctors he met as friends. That while feeling certain of the implications so deeply he was able to smother them in veils of scintillating fun is a trick of the true comic genius. It is almost too successful for his purpose—the comedy tilts at the windmills of medical incompetence with all the *panache* of Don Quixote and hardly more of his destructive force.

In part this is due to the character of Louis Dubedat, the artist sacrificed to B.B.'s portentous stupidity. For Shaw has deliberately built his "dilemma" on the question as to whether Dubedat, a blackguard artist of genius, is worth saving in comparison with the hardworking Dr. Blenkinsop, no genius but of more practical use to society, and equally in need of the one hospital place available for Ridgeon's new cure for tuberculosis. Moreover, he clouds the issue with still another sideline—Sir Colenso Ridgeon's love for Dubedat's wife, which is in the end his less worthy consideration in abandoning Dubedat's case. All this is entertaining but tends to divert us from the original source of parody and real moral question.

Yet it is Dubedat, the artist, whose creed in the end becomes the focal point of the play; and, unscrupulous and Irishly irresponsible in life, he states it with unshaken, radiant faith in death:

> I believe in Michael Angelo, Velasquez and Rembrandt; in the might of design, the mystery of color, the redemption of all things by Beauty everlasting, and the message of Art that has made these hands blessed. Amen, Amen.

The suspicion lingers that Shaw liked this blackguard artist—whose blackguardliness at least involved bringing joy and color into drab lives and living for the moment; and Louis' impudent charm and gaiety owe much, it is obvious, to Shaw's knowledge of the Irish temperament as well as Irish irresponsibility. He is a gift to the actor of the right temperament, Granville-Barker being the original and the Irish actor, Cyril Cusack, a notable more recent portrayer: Cusack digging below the iridescent, mocking, bohemian surface to the artist of integrity and almost spiritual passion beneath it.

"The character of Dubedat illustrates one of my pet theses," wrote Shaw, "which is that no man is scrupulous all round. He has, according to his faculties and interests, certain points of honor, whilst in matters that do not interest him he is careless and unscrupulous. . . .When Dubedat says on his deathbed that he has fought the good fight, he is quite serious. He means that he has not painted little girls playing with fox terriers to be exhibited and sold at the Royal Academy, instead of doing the best he could in his art. . . .He had his faith, and upheld it."

It is a flaw in Jennifer that her love is too blind and too egoistic to accept the whole Louis; as Shaw paints her, to know the truth would be to destroy both her faith and her love—in fact, her world. Is it because of this that Jennifer, for all Shaw's assurances as to her Cornish passionate temperament, strikes us as cold, a less living and believable character altogether—and in some ways basically less likable—than the feckless but artistically courageous and unshakeable Louis? Something is missing here, not merely in Jennifer, but in Shaw, who presents her as a genuine example of a woman deeply in love with an artist and attempting to help him in every way possible in his work. Her minimizing of his faults is one thing, and shows natural loyalty; but Shaw's theory is that her blindness to their more serious nature is a real blindness, and her love therefore founded on an illusion, unable to survive its destruction. In other words, Louis must fit her preconceived concept of the artist and person *she* would like to love, wholly devoted to herself and her image of him.

But this, though there are many cases of it accepted as "love" the world over (and it is often to be found in the wives of men of talent), is not genuine love but possessiveness born of egoism, as possessiveness always is; and it is a distinction between Ibsen and Shaw as dramatists and psychologists that Ibsen would instantly have seen this (witness Hjalmar Ekdal), while Shaw did not. With Louis and his genius he was altogether more clearsighted, and successful where many inferior writers have failed. "Probably it needs genius to paint genius," I wrote in a chapter on Shaw in *Theatre of Two Decades*; "and though the art may be of another kind, the springs of genius have a common fount."

The Doctor's Dilemma in 1906 was the last major play of Shaw's written for and produced at the Royal Court. The theatre had served its purpose, and Shaw, whose business sense had been exceptionally percipient throughout the whole venture, was the first to see this and point out its inevitability to Barker in a letter of April 21, 1907, when the suggestion of Barker's taking over the management of the larger West End theatre, the Savoy, was in the air: "The game is up at the Court: it has not yet begun at the Savoy. Four years is enough to give any one move in the way of high art. . .Debating societies, which always begin on a wave of public interest in something, begin to die after four years; and the Court is nothing but a debating society. The Shaw boom, in its novelty phase, cannot last longer."

Shaw's sound sense in all such matters was never disturbed by any personal considerations of conceit or egoism as an artist, and his letters to Barker throughout the association dealt with the business side with unfailing and painstaking understanding. He knew by now all aspects of the theatre, practical and artistic; and was certainly no mere "study" writer sitting back and waiting for others to interpret his works according to their own lights and abilities. It was here at the Royal Court that he developed his *flair* as a director—although Barker was in most cases officially in control of rehearsals and staging—by sitting at rehearsals taking meticulous notes, all of supreme value to the actors, as were his own inimitable gifts in that direction in demonstrating a point.

Sir Lewis Casson, who was in the company at the Royal Court and the first Octavius in *Man and Superman*, has written most revealingly of Shaw's rehearsal style:

> In his whole history as a producer of his own or anyone else's plays, I never knew Shaw take any serious practical interest in anything beyond the casting and acting. All the rest, including scenery, costumes, lighting and grouping, was of very minor importance, and personally, as a director, I sympathise with him. His printed stage directions manoeuvre his characters so that each speaker is fully seen and well lit, and as, in his plays, attention is almost always on the speaker rather than the listener, this simple rule usually suffices. . . .
>
> Before this season, the only two directors of note I had seen at work were Charles Fry and William Poel, both skilled hands in Shakespeare; and admiring the mastery of G.B.S. in *John Bull's Other Island* I had no idea then how very little

experience of direction he had actually had. And so it did not seem to me such a miracle as it might to see old stalwarts like Louis Calvert and John L. Shine, both masters of their craft and directors themselves of vast experience, not merely meekly, but enthusiastically, accepting Shaw's detailed direction. He could not, at that time, have directed more than three or four productions, almost all for private performance. How did he manage it? First, I suppose, because good actors at once recognize and respect a good actor (even if they dislike him, an impossibility in this case), and Shaw was a mighty good actor. Whether he could have carried a characterization through a whole evening, I don't know, but in giving a vivid half-minute sketch of a character as a demonstration, I know few better. So his suggestions to any other good actor on how a character would react, always rang true and were readily accepted.

He gives, too, an interesting picture of Shaw at this time, blossoming in his first real public theatrical success: "He must then have been about forty-eight, but he looked much younger; his hair and beard still flaming red, his eyes bubbling with merriment and mischief, with a boyish apologetic chuckle, almost a giggle, at his own jokes, a ready roar at anyone else's. A long lanky figure, with an easy springy stride like a hunting dog."[3]

Gilbert Murray, who for obvious reasons also watched at the Court, reinforces Casson. "He was, of course, a beautiful producer. No rehearsal was ever stale or dull. He never spared people's feelings and never hurt them, either, because he somehow established an atmosphere in which one knew that all the worst was openly said, and nothing but friendliness and good will left behind. . . What a treat it was to hear him read! There was first the delicate variety of tone, but still more there was the rollicking boyish enjoyment of his own jokes. On one occa-

[3] "A Tribute to George Bernard Shaw, 1856-1950." *Drama*, the Quarterly Theatre Review issued by the British Drama League, Summer, 1951.

sion long afterwards, when by ordinary human standards he was an old man, I heard him reading *Too True To Be Good*, and commented on his boyish vividness, and he said, 'Oh, second childhood!' It was a childhood that never left him."[4]

Throughout the Court seasons, Shaw bombarded Barker with letters and interested himself particularly in the casting of the plays, on which subject his comments were devastating and, one senses, completely sound. Not for nothing had he been a critic and seen the best and worst acting both the straight theatre and opera could offer over a period of many years. It was a theory of his that if the play were *cast* right, meaning the actors were all basically suited to their roles, the rest did not greatly matter: otherwise all Barker's own ingenuity of grouping and stage "business" could not save the production from misfiring. Where his own plays were concerned this was fundamentally sound; the words and characters in Shaw are of primary importance. And it is truer of many other dramatists than the modern emphasis on visual effect in theatre staging sometimes realizes.

Shaw was not a great sympathizer with Gordon Craig, that wayward imaginative genius whose brain-children never achieved wide practical fulfillment in his own country, though they influenced stage design throughout the world; and it is doubtful today if he would be any more sympathetic to the equally revolutionary but more practical symbolic staging by Wieland and Wolfgang Wagner of their grandfather's operas at Bayreuth, unless the casting and singing again perfectly met with Shaw's own exacting requirements. To some kinds of genius Shaw was strangely immune, in spite of his wide knowledge of pictures gained as art critic and frequenter of art galleries; and there is no reason to suspect he was in the least influenced

[4] *Ibid.*

by Craig's constantly shown hatred and denigration of him, for he wrote of him with personal forbearance and even understanding on several occasions. (Craig's jealousy of his mother's supposed subservience to Shaw, and passionate partisanship of Henry Irving, his idol when he was a young actor in his company, made him completely unbalanced in all his writings on Shaw.)

The correspondence with Barker continued for many years afterwards, only dying out after Barker's divorce from Lillah McCarthy, and marriage to his second wife, Helen, an American society woman who hated his connection with the theatre and all his theatre friends, Shaw in particular. Lillah had appealed to Shaw during Granville's period of entanglement with Helen, and her vast unhappiness, and long fight to save her marriage, distressed him no less than his sense of the fact that his own feelings, too, must be wounded by this new alliance. His letters to her did all they could in common sense and human understanding, and in the end, for Granville's sake, he advised her to accept the inevitable. But Barker had come to stand to him and Charlotte in the nature of a son—so much so, indeed, that St. John Ervine quotes an unfounded rumor that the young man was actually Shaw's true illegitimate son—and this breach was to prove for him the most bitter and hurtful in his personal relationships.

The truth is Barker liked luxury, which his new wife was able amply to provide for him, and not loath to sever his practical connection with the theatre for writing. His own plays—not works of genius like Shaw's, or even as dramatically important as John Galsworthy's, but good "plays of ideas"—had been a feature of the Court seasons; but in retirement his major work was really his *Prefaces to Shakespeare,* volumes of immense practical illumination to the actor and director. In 1940 he came briefly out of retirement to part-direct with Lewis Casson an Old Vic revival of *King Lear,* still memorable for its revelation of character and its magnificent performance of Lear by John Gielgud, himself a Barker enthusiast.

Otherwise, he severed his connection with the world of the theatre completely: a strange, enigmatic man who if he had regrets never showed them to anyone, and seemed entirely and one would say heartlessly untouched by the grief and affection he left behind him. The very mental attributes that attracted Shaw to him became the sharp knives that turned and pierced the older man. For Shaw beneath the shell was softer than men realized, like many whose compassion goes deep and must be projected through apparent cynicism and laughter.

His last communication to Barker, on September 14, 1943, was an announcement on a postcard of his wife's death: "Charlotte died last Sunday, the 12th September, at half past two in the morning. She had not forgotten you." And it ended, like a poignant period to past friendship, after long silence: "It was a blessedly happy ending; but you could not have believed I should be as deeply moved. You will not, I know, mind my writing this to you. She was 86. I am 87. G.B.S."

Barker died in Paris on August 31, 1946. Shaw heard the news at his home at Ayot St. Lawrence, quite without warning, on the B.B.C. Home Service News. The attachment was still deep enough to cost him a pang, although the golden young actor and associate of his earliest success was sixty-eight years of age, and they had not met for many years. It was perhaps because of this, even more than Charlotte's death, that Shaw at last showed signs of having lost interest in life.

Chapter 8

War and Peace and Mrs. Pat

IN PERIOD OF time, Shaw's love affair with the actress Mrs. Patrick Campbell reached its height on the fringes of the First World War, and therefore at the end of England's century of peace at least as regards a major European war. Nature could not have timed it more appropriately; and if War and Peace in the Tolstoyan sense apply to the direction of Shaw's work in these years, in the domestic sense the description is no less apt. For these were his own years of private conflagration and tempest, and the remarkable thing is that in the circumstances his work did not suffer more.

In fact, he was feverishly active, as his letters to her show; committees, suffragette and wartime, pepper his restless pages, no less than theatre business and the endless worries of production and royalties. (Shaw's stern hold on the business reins was at least as large a factor as actual genius in his success, and his taking of Mrs. Pat's chaotic affairs in hand might have been the saving of a less hopelessly mercurial and spendthrift, though acquisitive, personality.)

At the same time, there is a waning in his creative work: fewer plays, certainly, than in the heart of the Court Theatre activities, and none except *Androcles and the Lion* and *Pygmalion* (designed for Mrs. Pat) that seem in the major line of his composition and thought. In a sense this was inevitable. The brief flowering of the Court Theatre and close association with Barker provided that kind of stimulus most valuable to the artist, and most of all the theatre artist, always bedeviled by doubts about finding a producer and an audience. Shaw for the first time was in a position where he could count on the production of any play he cared to write: working, moreover, in association with congenial minds and with a friend and actor, young Barker, whose gifts he knew he could use to advantage, as Barker could use his own. The end of the Court was not the end of the association, which came indeed much later; but Barker's interest at the Savoy Theatre and elsewhere took a new direction, towards Shakespeare, and his productions now were to set the seal on his classical reputation as a director. Shaw knew this, and did not quibble; but the knowledge left his own creativity less sure of its eventual outlet, and less urgently needed.

The explosion of his interest in Mrs. Pat brought his whole creative activity, if not to a standstill, at least momentarily under a cloud. In spite of popular myth, creative art does not thrive in the midst of the mental and emotional upsets of affairs of the heart that are not going easily or according to plan; though the backwash later, when the worst has passed, may stir up a new creative sensibility, "emotion recollected in tranquillity" as Wordsworth described it. For Shaw, this meant *Heartbreak House,* believed by himself to be his greatest play and, though begun early in the Mrs. Pat affair, long in completion. But the desert that preceded it cannot only be explained by the First World War and Shaw's journalistic work in connection with his campaign (as always) against official humbug and red tape concerning it.

In the interim between *The Doctor's Dilemma,* the last outstanding Shaw play under the Barker-Vedrenne management at the Court Theatre, and *Pygmalion,* first produced in London on April 11, 1914, Shaw's principal plays were *Getting Married, Misalliance,* a shorter one, *The Shewing-Up of Blanco Posnet, Fanny's First Play* (written for and presented by Lillah McCarthy at the Little Theatre in 1911 and the Kingsway Theatre in 1912—

where its 622 performances gave it the longest single run enjoyed by a Shaw play), and *Androcles and the Lion.* The rest were one-act plays all written for a purpose but of no lasting value except possibly for *The Dark Lady of the Sonnets,* still sometimes performed as an interesting comment on Shakespeare, his mysterious "dark lady," and Queen Elizabeth, a part in any play always attractive to leading actresses.

Getting Married was produced by the Barker-Vedrenne management at the Haymarket Theatre for a two-weeks' season of matinees in 1908; and being a sensible disquisition (Shaw called it "a Disquisitory Play") on marriage aroused the usual outraged protest of post-Victorian opinion. In fact, Shaw's suggestion of a seven-year agreement binding on both parties, subject to ratification or dissolution later according to how it had worked in practice, was ironically shown in the play to be just as hazardous in the working as the more normal arrangement in so highly unpredictable a state as the cohabitation under law of two diverse human beings. Our modern laws accepting divorce are more sensible (especially in the United States where ordinarily they do not, as still in England, enforce adultery on one party), and Shaw like most reformers was merely ahead of public opinion in common sense and his refusal to idealize an often frankly unromantic and even mercenary business. The bitter harvest in human misery (including the children) of an irrevocable alliance between people ill-assorted and quite often in youth unable to know each other's true character—victims, moreover, in many cases of a deliberate deceit in this respect on one side—could not be expected to have sanction on the dubious grounds of "religion" in a mind as questioning and rational as Shaw's. Where social and religious considerations conflict, he would be expected to side with the social. On the other hand, the durability of his own marriage—even under a stress as great as that soon afterwards imposed on it by his infatuation for Mrs. Pat—proves he was no irresponsible hedonist in this sense, and only too conscious of the loyalties involved in any union undertaken and sustained with reasonable contentment by both parties. His own religion was not orthodox, but it embraced the genuine and important humanities; and that these sometimes conflicted with rules set up by the Church was for him something to be recognized frankly, not ignored.

In *The Shewing-Up of Blanco Posnet* (1909), which he subtitled "A Sermon in Crude Melodrama," the religious direction of his thought became more marked; and the play was in fact originally banned for public performance by a censor scandalized—as Beerbohm Tree, the actor for whom it was written, had been—by Blanco's bitter line about God's being "a sly one," "a mean one," who "plays cat and mouse with you." The fact that this is direct and believable characterization in a renegade against society was no help to Shaw: the belief that everything put by a creative writer into the mouth of one of his characters represents his own personal view on any given subject is a long-standing one, enjoyed by most readers and even some critics, and Shaw made his position harder in this case by obviously preferring the blasphemous Blanco, on trial for his life for horse stealing, to the sanctimonious but morally un-Christian community that condemned him. That the comedy still holds the stage was shown in 1961 when it was successfully staged by Bernard Miles' enterprising management at the new Mermaid Theatre on London's Thames Embankment, in a double "bill" with *Androcles and the Lion:* thus happily coupling the "Sermon" and the "Fable" of Shaw's dramatic aspects of religion in daily life.

Androcles and the Lion was the more deeply serious play, a conflagration perhaps flaring up from a spark thrown up by *Blanco Posnet*. One of the theatre's most popular melodramas in Victorian and Edwardian times had been *The Sign of the Cross,* known in theatres throughout the world following its production by the romantic actor-manager, Wilson Barrett. *Androcles* was, as might be expected from Shaw, its antidote and antithesis, yet despite its pantomimic aspects by far the more profound and serious play, in the religious no less than the dramatic sense.

It was written in part, Shaw told his biographer Hesketh Pearson, as a balance to children's plays such as Barrie's *Peter Pan,* which he insisted (and maintained Max Beerbohm had proved in a caricature reading of the Barrie play) were more enjoyable to adults than to children. It was written "to show what a play for children should be like. It should never be childish; nothing offends children more than to play down to them; all the great children's books, *The Pilgrim's Progress, Gulliver, Robinson Crusoe,* Andersen, *Arabian Nights,* and Grimms' *Fairy Tales,* were written for adults."

Certainly children in the audience enjoy *Androcles and the Lion,* in particular of course the scenes with the lion, which is a part an actor-mime of talent can make specially endearing. But its core is far beyond them, being an unraveling of the psychological forces which make men and women embrace martyrdom. Shaw was quick to see these differed from individual to individual, and could be quite outside the beliefs themselves, even the belief of immortality and heavenly reward. A Ferrovius is always on the verge of the un-Christian gesture of "hitting back"—in fact slaying his persecutors as enthusiastically as a veritable follower of Mars—just as a Lavinia cannot put her instinct to rational discourse, feeling only that death rather than acquiescence in a lie is something her nature and her moral precepts demand that she face, with dignity and without even special vilification of the other side. There are, too, the Spinthos who take to martyrdom as a kind of self-glorification, and having no deep inner convictions outside it can only turn tail and flee (straight, in this case, into the lion's jaws) when put to the test.

Androcles himself, the "little man" confronted with a faith bigger than himself, and therefore to be followed with humility to whatever end, is perhaps an echo of Wagner's "guileless Fool"—*"der Reine Tor"*—Parsifal, but a Parsifal who never grows out of childhood into a man of mature wisdom, fit guardian of the Holy Grail. Tending the lion with the thorn in his paw (perhaps an allegorical parallel of the Good Samaritan story?), and in the Roman arena reaping the just reward for his charity when the beast recognizes and refuses to eat him, Androcles is close to Shaw's heart as a vegetarian and lover of animals, with a petting "baby talk" meant surely (it has irritated some pontifical critics) to point the closeness to childhood of the purest form of a religion which has, as a key phrase: "Suffer the little children to come unto Me, for of such is the Kingdom of Heaven."

It was not, perhaps, inappropriate that in Shaw's native Dublin the play chosen by Cyril Cusack to honor his centenary was *Androcles and the Lion*; for this simple parable has at its heart some of the best of Shaw, morally and philosophically. Its original production was at the St. James's Theatre, London, on September 1, 1913, with a distinguished cast including Lillah McCarthy as Lavinia, a part that was written for her.

During 1912 and 1913 Shaw was writing *Pygmalion*, this time with Mrs. Patrick Campbell in mind as his leading lady. Their correspondence had begun rather desultorily some years before regarding *Caesar and Cleopatra*, in which it had proved impossible to bring her into conjunction with the intended Caesar, Forbes-Robertson. Efforts to arrange a two-star constellation with Robert Loraine, a favorite actor of Shaw's who had played John Tanner at the Court Theatre, proved equally abortive. And when her Eliza Doolittle was eventually successfully teamed with the Professor Higgins of the great actor-manager Tree, Shaw must have been as surprised and relieved as anybody, in spite of his capitulation by now to the charms of the lady. For in Mrs. Patrick Campbell the English stage had thrown up one of its rare actresses of genuine temperament; one, moreover, who had begun somewhat as a society amateur and dilettante and whose lack of professionalism—in its narrower sense—in the end turned her into one of the great eccentrics of our theatre, whose eccentricity and self-absorption were her own undoing. "She had the world at her feet," as Shaw wrote. "But she kicked the ball away, and it rolled out of her reach."

Yet she was a creature of extraordinary beauty, of Italian blood and with eyes, as Shaw once described those of her daughter in his unromantic but vivid idiom, like "blackberry jam." And more important than beauty, she was an actress of natural, undisciplined genius, with that corollary which every successful player in some degree must possess, a personality so magnetic, and basically so sexually attractive, that it hypnotizes not only in the theatre but outside it. Rereading his earlier reviews of her performances, at the height of his passion for her, Shaw found to his surprise (and relief, for he did not hesitate to write to her of the discovery) that already, although he was unaware of it, her irresistible attraction for him was discernible, and though he slaughtered the plays she appeared in, it was only to heighten the triumphant radiance of her performances (perversely, like most players, she had remembered across the years only critical pinpricks, none of the lavished praise).

But over this business of getting *Pygmalion* produced, years later, they began to meet, and a correspondence commenced no less intimate than Shaw's with Ellen Terry but infinitely more passionate in its implications. Shaw, for the only time in his life, was swept off his feet, and acknowledged the fact wrily enough to himself both at the time and (with unusual male honesty) later.

I drove into Dublin today and cursed every separate house as I passed. All the old longing for beauty and blessing gets stirred up in me; and as I come back into the country you are no longer that popular actress Mrs. Bella Donna,[1] but my girl, my beauty, my darling, barefooted, dusty petticoated, or my mother of angels, or a dozen lovely wild things that would greatly astonish the young lions of the St. James's stalls. . . .
So if you are idly curious as to whether I am still in love with Stella, the answer is yes yes yes yes yes yes yes yes yes yes yes yes yes yes yes yes yes yes yes yes yes yes yes yes yes yes yes and a million times yes. Cannot help it. Am quite sensible, quite able, quite myself, and yet a lad playing with you on the mountains and unable to feel where you begin and I leave off.

Do not suppose, however, that I do not know that you are a great and wonderful woman, and so beautiful that all the stars are not too fine to make a necklace for you, and that there are secret places in the world where there is nobody else but you.

Yet here I am caught up again, hearthless, with no foothold, at a dizzy height, in an ecstasy which must be delirious and presently end in my falling headlong to destruction. And yet I am happy, as madmen are. What does this sound like from me, the supersane man? I am not otherwise mad; yet I am stark raving mad in this matter unless you are indeed and in truth an extraordinary person, a genius, a half goddess, wonderfully lovely, wonderfully tender, and simply sincere and pitiful and—Oh for the word: I am at last at a loss for one—when you take me up and say. . . . I can't write those words: they can exist only in my holiest memory now.
And this—*this* you have done by a couple of days' silence, a couple of days' hunger, a couple of days' brazen descent in-

[1] *Bella Donna* was the title of the play in which Mrs. Pat was appearing, as a *femme fatale* and murderess. Years later Pola Negri acted the part in a film.

to an accustomed despair, and at the end, a scrawl—a little whisper of poetry and petting and thrushes and the like. Oh Stella, Stella, Stella, Stella, I no longer regret anything; so take care, take care. . .

I don't know why; I can't write. Writing is no use. I have written everything, said everything. And I am saying it still. Only, I want to say it so that you can really feel it.

Did she "really feel it?" She was flattered, of course, and *Pygmalion* was a dazzling bait. Improvident as always, sometimes ill, a creature of nerves and magic born of that mystery and changeability of mood that always, allied to beauty, create magic in a woman for men, she sent back little sparkling spiders'-web threads of enticement, wit and high intelligence (all necessary to captivate a Shaw, never the kind of intelligent man to demand and accept foolishness in women). But what she really felt for him, how much indeed of herself she actually yielded, remains something of an enigma. One senses a holding back, and when the actual crisis towards which the relationship was obviously moving came, and Shaw followed her to her retreat at Sandwich by the sea, she fled, after sending in vain a note brief with alarm: "Please will you go back to London to-day—or go wherever you like but dont stay here—If you wont go I must—I am very very tired and I oughtn't to go another journey. Please dont make me despise you. Stella."

When he reached the hotel, another even briefer note announced her departure.

His own letters (one headed "Sandwich. Darkness. 11th August 1913") were cries of genuine, wounded rage; including a sense, too (it is a clue, in such a man, to the genuineness of both the hurt and his affection), of his own inadequacy in some way with regard to her. "Very well, go; the loss of a woman is not the end of the world. The sun shines; it is pleasant to swim; it is good to work; my soul can stand alone. But I am deeply, deeply, deeply wounded. You have tried me; and you are not comfortable with me; I cannot bring you peace, or rest, or even fun. . . ."

Even here, he cannot keep to seriousness long. The letters and friendship had begun with a certain amount of Irish "blarney," deliberate coquetry on both sides and understood as such, for a business purpose (*Pygmalion*). And the scorching reality into which Shaw suddenly found himself thrust by a heart less steeled than he had thought it was a kind of warning by Nature that we cannot so easily civilize her instinctive processes. The same letter makes an attempt to return to the earlier style:

> I have treated you too well, idolized, thrown my heart and mind to you (as I throw them all to the world) to make what you could of; and what you make of them is to run away. Go then: the Shavian oxygen burns up your little lungs. . . . You have wounded my vanity: an inconceivable audacity, an unpardonable crime.
>
> Farewell, wretch that I loved. G.B.S.

But the same day another letter—"Sandwich. Darkness" —flew with burning wings after the first: "Oh my rancor is not yet slaked; I have not said enough vile things to you. What are you, miserable wretch, that my entrails should be torn asunder hour after hour? Of that 57 years I have suffered 20 and worked 37. Then I had a moment's happiness: I almost condescended to romance. I risked the breaking of deep roots and sanctified ties; I set my feet boldly on all the quicksands: I rushed after Will o' the Wisp into darkness: I courted the oldest illusions, knowing well what I was doing. I seized handfuls of withered leaves and said 'I accept them for gold.' And now there is that desolate strand, and the lights of Ramsgate that might have been the camp fires of the heavenly hosts on the Celestial mountains. . . ."

And much later, after more in this strange Celtic poetic

vein that seemed suddenly—part simulated, part irrepressibly real—to surge up in Shaw's prose in this last and almost only Irish madness of his life, the real hurt emerges and reasserts itself: "It is I who cared, you who didn't. That is as becomes me. I no longer look up to the queen of heaven: I tower mountainous to the skies and see a pretty little thing wondering at me. How is it that this infinitesimal nothingness yet drags at my midriff and causes me strange pangs and makes me write wild nonsense?"

And so it went on. He fled back to his work—but wrote "the wound will not heal." "Do you think it was nothing to me," she had written, "to hurt my friend—." He was still her "dear Joey," and she strove hard to tie together the strings of a broken friendship. (". . . she would tear the strings out of an archangel's harp to tie up parcels," he had written: "she has done that with my very heartstrings.") In fact, as he knew, she had become engaged to George Cornwallis-West, who became her second husband the following spring within a few days of the production of *Pygmalion;* and half in banter, half earnest, he had compared the difference in their ages and pointed out that he had only a few years to give her; George, the much younger man (whom he liked), had time on his side: "so let him wait until I am tired of you." Perhaps it was this sense of urgency of his that brought his pursuit to the boil.

But there was more to it, one suspects, than this—Shaw was becoming a danger to her remarriage, without himself for one moment suggesting the barest possibility of his leaving Charlotte, and, a woman whose caprices and lack of business temperament always made single life financially difficult, she may well have felt her heart betraying her into some deeper attachment which would pass, and leave her high and dry on some barren shore. Shaw's biographer, St. John Ervine, who hated her, can see in her only some heartless, acquisitive *femme fatale* out of the mid-Victorian theatre; but it is patently a biased and inhuman portrait which does not accord with some of the obviously genuine patches in her letters, her occasional thoughtless generosities, her emotional splendors as an actress, her quick sympathy in bereavement, and her capacity of affection for her two children. The son, "Beo," was killed a few years later in the First World War, and Shaw was one of the first to send her words of comfort in what he, of all people, knew to be her deep and genuine grief. As for her mind, which Ervine venomously derides, it had a spark in it that could ignite Shaw's own, and her defense of Ibsen's Hedda Gabler against his more astringent interpretation, in some proofs he had sent her to read,[2] shows her feeling for the emotion of the women she presented on the stage had understanding and compassion behind it.

> But your "Hedda" makes me very sad—not one little bit do you understand Hedda — your interpretation of "do it beautifully" positively made me scream—her love—her shame —her physical condition—her agonizing jealousy—even the case of pistols—you're wrong on all points—did you think about it at all—or is it just your adoration for bl——y plain facts that makes you so indifferent to all the poetry, the universal truths and beauty that lie behind and beyond?—You miss it all dolefully in *Little Eyolf*—the fact is you write carelessly sometimes—And with whom are you quarrelling? Be calm dearest, be gentle with fools—And why take it for granted that your reader doesn't know what you know, and isn't agreeing with you?
>
> You seem to have a simpleton always in your mind's eye. . . . The fact is you have too much brain—you tumble up against it—I admit my heart thrills as you bravely "get there" —but oh my, you do turn such inadvised St. Catherine Wheels! . . . If one wasn't afraid of your turning Catherine Wheels in one's heart, how one would adore you . . .
>
> I knew by instinct what Ibsen and the rest of them *taught* you—But then I had a father who only read and talked Dar-

[2] Presumably the 1913 new revised edition of *The Quintessence of Ibsenism*.

win, and a mother who loved only Dante—and whose soul was steeped in beauty.

This is not only percipient criticism of Shaw, which he was openminded enough to relish, but a clue to the woman as well as the actress herself. It was, in fact, a key to her fascination for him. As she says, he was not gentle with fools, and it needed far more than a physical passion to bind such a man in such chains as, for a long period, she forged for him. No physical passion can drive such deep wounds into such a soul, or indeed in any soul. His conception of her may have been part illusion, as he admitted in the toils; but it was fact too, as her letters prove, and some of it remained undimmed through all the begging letters, the valiant self-justification, the soul-wrecking poverty yet at times flash of undefiled memory of her later years. When they were both old, she became an embarrassment, not the least in her urgent requests that he should allow her to publish his letters to her; for her temperament that had closed many stages to her, with her fading beauty, had left her in dire need of money. Her magic for him had lingered long after her marriage, in a continued correspondence and long friendship, and to the end, though he scolded, he never was quite able to throw her off. But on the question of the letters he was adamant, for Charlotte's sake, and they never were published in her lifetime, although under a stipulation of Shaw's their proceeds went eventually to her great grandchildren, for their education.

Where, in fact, did Charlotte stand in all this? One letter of Shaw's is explicit enough: it was written in May, 1913, several months before the Sandwich crisis, following a telephonc conversation with Mrs. Pat that Charlotte had unfortunately overheard.

I am all torn to bits: you don't know what it is to me to be forced to act artificially when everything has been freshly stirred in me. It gives me a sort of angina pectoris. . . .

But the worst of it is that all our conversation was overheard; and the effect was dreadful: it hurts me miserably to see anyone suffer like that. I must, it seems, murder myself or else murder her. . . .

Well, I dare say it is good for us all to suffer; but it is hard that the weak should suffer the most. If I could be human and suffer with a suffering of my own, there would be some poetic justice in it; but I cant; I can only feel the sufferings of others with a pain that pity makes, and with a fierce impatience of the unreasonableness of it—the essential inhumanity of this jealousy that I never seem able to escape from. And it is a comfort at least that you also have the unquenchable gaiety of genius, and can stand anything.

Perhaps she could; but perhaps, too, she began to wonder, faced with this apparent inability to suffer and this constitutional reluctance, for all his unconventional theories, to break a marriage which was unromantic on his side and yet a close companionship with a person he could not bring himself to hurt by a final parting. The suffering, for him, came later—he was more vulnerable than he thought—and too late. And in an earlier letter he had probably not staved off his fate by describing to Mrs. Pat a rally of Charlotte's—Irish, too, by birth and therefore unstable enough in her moods—which certainly must have suggested to her rival she had some cause for confidence in the saving of her marriage:

Charlotte has suddenly got well, and changed from a fiend into a green-eyed mermaid, smiling and fascinating and dressing in diamonds and generally dispensing charm and childish happiness. What is more amazing, she actually refers to you without fury, even with raillery. "Did you go to Brighton that day at Beachy Head?" Boundless contempt for both of us; but no more hatred, almost a joyous contempt. . . . Dont grudge her her contempt; for the difference between that and the sick hatred and fury her illness produced is for me the difference between heaven and hell. She cannot, like you, laugh through her last gasp.

Laugh or not, it was not reassuring to a woman in love; and if Mrs. Pat was not that she certainly showed many genuine signs of being on the brink, with a tenderness to her "Joey" which to some extent outlasted the years. How can one tell what truly lay behind the laughing mask Shaw himself (perhaps prompted by Charlotte, whose jealousy does not seem likely to have made her scrupulous) had fashioned for her? If she was hurt, too, she hid it, but the memory of Charlotte's radiant recovery is not likely to have left her. If she ran away to escape further hurt, not only she was to blame.

The final triumph was Charlotte's, who had won Shaw not by love but by her own initiative and the good luck in having the wealth to cross a continent to him when his physical resources were at their weakest; and she is not greatly to be pitied, for the wealthy, for whom everything is made easy from birth, have a personal star of fortune which tends not to forsake them but follow them through life. The "haves" of this world often retain what they desire for they have the means to do so reinforced by the desperate fear of losing it. Mrs. Pat had only the resources of her beauty and charm, which are not ageless; she may have squandered them, and become the victim of her own reckless temperament and character, but the lack of a "business" head, though disastrous, is not entirely an unsympathetic characteristic. What money she had, she had to earn, by her talents or through marriage; and the first is never easy for a woman alone in any society. For all Ervine's criticism of her callous calculation, her ruinous later life did not subscribe to such an assessment. Those who squander—in generosity or emotion—do not count the cost; and whatever cost had to be paid, in the end Stella Campbell paid in full.

She died, very poor, in Paris in 1940, at the age of seventy-five. "Yes, she is dead," wrote Shaw, "and everybody is greatly relieved; herself, I should say, most of all;

for the last pictures of her are not those of a happy woman. She was not a great actress but she was a great enchantress, how or why I don't know; but if she wanted to capture you, you might as well go quietly; for she was irresistible. . . . She did not know how to live with real people in the real world. She was a hybrid, half Italian, half suburban Croydon; and the transition from one to the other was bewildering. Though her grandfather ran a circus and her mother rode in it and was never anglicized, there must have been a strain of nobility on the Italian side; for she could behave finely on occasion. She enchanted me among the rest; but I could not have lived with her for a week; and I knew it; so nothing came of it."

The final implication was what Shaw in old age perhaps wanted to believe; but the Sandwich letters give it the lie. His masculine pride, and in this matter he had some, concealed the fact that the real truth of the matter was she had jilted *him*, and his natural reaction had been that of all those who realize the true value of a possession only when they have lost it. His assumption that they could not have lived together for a week without combustion is possibly true; but it is an afterthought and a consolation, even though he may have sensed it instinctively at the time.

Peace, through Mrs. Pat, therefore ended for Shaw with an explosion: the last deeply personal crisis of his long life. *Pygmalion*, for all its subsequent fame (not the least as the musical *My Fair Lady*, about Shaw's possible reactions to which one must reserve judgment), was in the nature of a postscript to the affair, with Shaw the author reasserting himself tc bully, cajole and flatter her into a performance which he knew to be highly necessary to the success of the play. And it was certainly not without its technical difficulties for her, as she was professional enough to be aware; for she was a woman forty-eight years old, with grown-up children, and long past the age of the flower girl Eliza. She triumphed, no less than

Beerbohm Tree as Higgins, and thus won immortality in one of the most beguiling if not difficult parts in classic modern comedy; for classic the play has obstinately become—perhaps through this basic challenge of human transformation through education and environment, with the implications of the sex war still murmuring beneath its relationships.

Higgins is the dedicated artist in his profession, unaware of the undercurrent until the object of his experiment shows itself human, a creation that like Count Frankenstein's no less than the sculptor Pygmalion's has developed a will and dignity of its own. Perhaps, like Shaw with Mrs. Pat, he is aware of the value of his creation only when he has lost it. He wants it back, but on his own terms, and establishes them still without realizing to the full that he has hurt a human soul no less proud and self-sufficient than his own. Eliza's rebellion carries an echo of Ibsen's Nora's, and though the door of Higgins' house is metaphorical she nevertheless slams it.

It was a Shavian ending, refusing to romanticize; though if he knew anything about Eliza and women at all he can hardly have been unaware that her rebellion was of the individual human spirit against an attraction sexual and mental, that sought to dominate it, and showed signs of doing so. The throwing of the slippers at Higgins' head is a clear enough physical reaction against not only subjugation in itself, but subjugation by the resisting male. It is typical of the more romantic *media* into which the play has been translated in modern times—the *media* of films and musical stage—that the door no longer slams even metaphorically and Eliza ends up happily with a triumphant although unreformed Higgins (Shaw in an epilogue had suggested she married Freddy).

One reason for its original notoriety, of course, Eliza's "not bloody likely," has left it; though it remains the only play in which a word now squandered indiscriminately throughout texts is used meticulously in connection with a comedy point of situation and character. Nevertheless, there were moments later when Shaw wished heartily that he had never included it, it seemed to divert attention so fatally from the real purposes of his play. The play is not his greatest; yet that it has become a classic of our comedy stage few would deny.

Produced at His Majesty's Theatre on April 11, 1914, it was Shaw's last serious work for the theatre until the end of the war; for *Heartbreak House*, in some ways his most serious play and his greatest in his own view, was not completed and produced until 1921, although he began it, prophetically, before the outbreak of war.

The English theatre in wartime produced mainly only frivolities, meant to cheer the soldiers on leave from the bloodiest and most wasteful war in history; and Shaw himself, wracked by his sense of war's futility and anger at its excesses, concentrated mainly on journalism, lost causes and pamphleteering, such as his *Common Sense about the War*: which put the nation into a patriotic ferment of vilification—and incidentally lost him many friends—though with its general criticism of the English government's policy (notably in plunging Europe into war by not warning the Kaiser more clearly that we would in fact fight if Belgium were invaded) most historians would agree today.

In 1913 he had supported H. W. Massingham in the founding of *The New Statesman and Nation*, a critical left wing journal which was to remain vigorous through two successive wars and will probably survive the third if and when it comes. For this he wrote regularly until his death, though in his last years mainly in its correspondence columns, where in a lively nonagenarian bout of arms he demolished a younger playwright, Terence Rattigan, among altogether more formidable undertakings. During the 1914-1918 War he also became involved in the treason trial of Roger Casement, taking a balanced view of the case (as compared with hysteria on both sides, for and against, which included among the first Beatrice Webb, who bitterly disliked and underrated Shaw in spite of his long association with Sidney, and particularly damned his efforts to bring reason into this case). He himself as a last resource to save Casement drafted a speech of defense for him at the trial which was never used, but certainly would have brought some sane reasoning into the matter had it been so.

His *Peace Conference Hints* of 1919 likewise contained a good deal of sense which has proved historically sound. But it is in the nature of prophets to be underrated and reviled because ahead of their time, and again his success was historical rather than immediate—and such successes are out-of-date before they are realized as such.

Shaw's lasting monument erected from the War was *Heartbreak House*, which through Hesione Hushabye reflects not for the last time the "radiance recollected in tranquillity" that was Mrs. Pat.

Begun before the War, this "Fantasia in the Russian Manner," as Shaw called it, derived in style from Tchekhov's painting of a society in decline, and swept away for ever by war and revolution. Shaw's sense that Edwardian society in England was similarly on the verge of dissolution was profound and prophetic, and if his country house characters have as much of Slav fecklessness and fatalism as of English *fin de siècle savoir faire* in the face of changing values, that was a value rather than a loss to the play. For there is a poetry and imagination in *Heartbreak House* one finds lacking in much of Shaw, a Celtic upsurge loosened in him perhaps, as it was loosened in his letters, by the impact of Mrs. Pat on his too-long-suppressed emotion and Irish heritage. Old Shotover's irresistible daughters are an obvious offshoot of his enthrallment with the actress, and rightly produced the last scene, in which they throb to the poetry of the dropping bombs and imagined fires, to the sound of Randall's violin, is a kind of threnody to the passing of all things bright and beautiful—like the sound of the axe destroying the cherry trees in *The Cherry Orchard.*

But the greatness of this play, for all its incidental coldnesses and cruelties and comic intrusions, is its oldest inhabitant, Captain Shotover, a figure rough-hewn out of his own poop like a figurehead on the prow of a ship, a King Lear without the tragedy (though certainly with hints of pathos) and still in spite of his calculated senile absent-mindedness in full command of his kingdom and his daughters. He is a prophet thundering in navigational terms of Britain's danger, but much more than that a prophet of war through the ages, now coming like a messenger of death, on wing, to destroy mankind.

It is its element of prophecy no less than its entertainment and liveliness of character that makes *Heartbreak House* whenever revived a play that seems to come with a new illumination, shedding light on whatever predicament mankind may at that time have found itself in. A revival at the Cambridge Theatre, London, in 1943, during World War II, with the fine actor Robert Donat as Shotover, seemed a searchlight on the time; and an equally successful production late in 1961 at Wyndham's Theatre—imaginatively produced by Frank Hauser, director of the enterprising Playhouse Theatre in Oxford—once again seemed to reflect the shadow of a new and even more destructive war falling like the wing of the angel of death over the world.

At the heart is human disillusion—the disillusion of love which finds its hardness in rebuilding a life without it, and its wisdom and resignation from the aged who have experienced all things, as Ellie does from Shotover. But there is valiancy, too, in the face of the bombs that suggests at the last the human will to survive, the Life Force still not spent. And in this the old Shaw thunders beneath the iridescent lightning of the future.

It is his work of purest imagination, in character and vision; and therefore his nearest to poetry, the highest expression of genius. By it, he lives on, dispelling wisdom and warning into the future. For this is a lion of a play, with a roar to waken the sleeping conscience of every generation.

Chapter 9

The Crown of Fame

Heartbreak House had first been presented by the Theatre Guild in New York on November 10, 1920, and its New York run of 125 performances was double that which it achieved in its first London production at the Royal Court Theatre—an association that must have stirred bittersweet memories in Shaw, though the manager was no longer Barker but J. B. Fagan. Fagan was an active man of the theatre who was responsible also for some notable Tchekhov revivals and the emergence at Oxford during the nineteen-twenties of some of the most brilliantly promising of England's actors and producers, among them Sir John Gielgud, Sir Tyrone Guthrie, Dame Flora Robson and others. Later at Oxford his production of the last scene of *Heartbreak House*—or at least the playing of it by the company at its last performance there, which Shaw attended—earned some devastating broadsides from its outraged author, who complained it had been played for laughs, not seriously as he had intended. But presumably this had been avoided in the original London production, when Fagan directed the play in conjunction with Shaw, and also designed the settings which, it would appear from extant photographs, were considerably below the artistic quality of those of the outstanding designer Lee Simonson for the American production.

Fagan, like H. K. Ayliff for many years at Malvern afterwards, probably well fitted the task of meeting Shaw's own main requirements, which, as we have seen, maintained that the visual effect was not important in comparison with the need to let the dialogue make its own point, with as little movement or fuss as possible. Shaw in this sense had his defects as a theatre director, though his basic point, the clearness of the discussion for intelligent assimilation by the audience, was very sound in connection with his own plays. Nevertheless, they might have gained much in England during his lifetime, and might still do so, from a more imaginative approach as regards staging. It is strange that Shaw had the intellectual vision and commonsensical theatre instinct to see, within a few years of Wagner's death, that any attempt to perpetuate the "Bayreuth tradition" he had established would mummify the operas rather than keep them alive and vigorous in future ages, while showing himself so little flexibility over a period of forty years with regard to the style of production of his own plays. Appreciating Gordon Craig so little, he is unlikely, one would say, to have recognized the extraordinary imaginative beauty and symbolic power of the design and production methods of Wieland Wagner in his grandfather's operas—revolutionary stagings which owe something to the influence of Craig on the European theatre. Perhaps understandably Shaw had not himself the original and creative artistic instinct which could foresee new methods of stylization in the theatre or rebel completely against the past. He could feel the need, at least in Wagner's case, but not envisage the form. In his own plays, in his lifetime, he "played safe," as far as he could, with direction and setting; and what could have made for extreme dullness—especially of pace, mobility and pictorial effect—in other plays never destroyed his own as long as they were well cast: which owing to his own *flair* and knowledge in the selection and assessment of actors was normally the case.

Nevertheless, both *Heartbreak House* and its colossal successor, *Back to Methuselah*, are plays with a deep symbolic core and significance (witness only the captain's poop old Shotover has erected to house his illusions and reinforce his symbol of navigational disaster), and their universal message and vision of humanity need expression through a style of staging less realistic, and infinitely wider in implication, than they normally get. *Back to Methuselah* also received its first production (in 1922) by the New York Theatre Guild, and once again the designs of Lee Simonson obviously surpassed those of the English production in imaginative composition and power: helped, it is apparent, by a use of stage lighting then hardly attempted in the English theatre. The English first production, it is true, was a repertory one; at Sir Barry Jackson's distinguished and experimental Birmingham Repertory Theatre, a year after the American production, followed by a season by the same company at the Royal Court Theatre in London. But the smallness of a theatre and its means has never precluded visual experiment in other countries, and of all plays *Back to Methuselah* is a gift to the Wieland Wagners of the theatre.

For this vast five-play cycle is Shaw's *Ring*; embracing not the fall of the gods and rise of the superman, but the creative evolution of man himself from the Garden of Eden to "As Far As Thought Can Reach," the title of the last play. Here human life has so mentally evolved that its method is oviparous, the child is born a fully equipped young adult, and ancients of eight hundred years walk the earth, all mind and skin and bone: supermen and superwomen in whom the power of thought alone has conquered the needs of mortality and the senses.

Being a throwback to the superman theme of Wagner and Nietzsche, it is also of course a new development in time of the ideas behind *Man and Superman*. In *Back to Methuselah*, Shaw wrote, "I abandon the legend of Don Juan with its erotic associations, and go back to the legend of the Garden of Eden." The theme he describes as "a second legend of Creative Evolution without distractions and embellishments," and "my beginning of a Bible for Creative Evolution." The intellectual and biological foundation of Shaw's view of human life—deriving from Lamarck in opposition to Darwin—is reiterated and expanded in a work which is in fact, as he says elsewhere, "a contribution to the modern Bible."

"It is a monument to human life and development from the Garden of Eden to As Far As Thought Can Reach, metaphysically allied to Schopenhauer's *The World as Will and Idea*," I wrote in *Theatre of Two Decades*. "Instead of the material barriers of Darwinism, which leave life helpless in the grip of accidental divergencies of natural selection, Shaw presents with Lamarck, the naturalist, and Schopenhauer, the philosopher, a view of human development based on direct application of will—the will to adapt itself, to evolve creatively, over centuries if need be, according to spiritual or physical need. We therefore have five plays, not one, showing the various phases of this creative evolution; beginning with Adam and Eve discovering the knowledge of mortality and reproduction; leaping to the present century and man's first vision of his power to increase the life-span; moving on to the situation two centuries later when the miracle (by quite unconscious will-power) has taken place and must be revealed; finally spanning aeons of time as the human race develops under its new momentum of long life and wisdom, until we work back at the end to Lilith, the creator of all life, soliloquising on man's vision of a future in which matter is eliminated in a vortex of thought.[1]

"The theme is one of heroic dimensions, outstripping Goethe and Milton in audacity. Has Shaw succeeded? No mental capacity of our time, certainly, would be large enough to succeed as well; which means, briefly, that Shaw

[1] The similarity of thought between this final great soliloquy in *Back to Methuselah* and Nina's famous speech in *The Seagull* (in Constantin's play) is striking. It would be interesting to know if Shaw was at all influenced by it.

has succeeded magnificently in parts, and falls short of genius in others through his inability not to play the fool. 'Seriousness is only a small man's affectation of business,' he once wrote: and certainly his wit, his buffoonery at times, are brilliant enough, and in their way relevant enough, to justify his use of them. In spite of its (at first sight) dated lampoons of Lloyd George and other politicians of the First World War, I am not, myself, ruffled unduly by the facetiousness of the second play, *The Gospel of the Brothers Barnabas*: political leaders have a habit of recurring in type, and most of Shaw's satire—like Gilbert's First Lord of the Admiralty, Sir Joseph Porter—remains pertinent today for this reason. The chief flaw in the drama is the fourth play, *The Tragedy of an Elderly Gentleman*, because it lacks integration in the whole and appears merely an irrelevant joke at the expense of Ireland and the British Empire. The long-livers here seem to have reverted merely to Delphic origins, and show so little of the accumulated wisdom we had sensed in their predecessors in the previous play that the Elderly Gentleman does, indeed, succeed in out-talking and out-thinking them on more than one occasion. There are sparkling moments, some good talk, but the play seems an irrelevant interlude.

"The genius—something at times very near to poetry—of the work lies predominantly in the first and last episodes, *In the Beginning* and *As Far As Thought Can Reach*, with the addition of some impressive moments of awe and tension in the third play, *The Thing Happens*, when we wait to see which of the characters we already know have actually achieved the longevity the Brothers Barnabas foresaw. In Adam and Eve's groping realization of the eternal facts of life—love, death and all the intermediaries of imagination and will—and their discovery of words to express them; in the Serpent's liquid tongue and secret wisdom; in the older Eve's simple description of the children and great grandchildren who 'cut reeds of different lengths and blow through them, making lovely patterns of sound in the air,' who 'tell beautiful lies in beautiful words,' and 'make little mammoths out of clay'; in Lilith's final great apostrophe on the human experiment—in these wonderful moments Shaw breaks through the bonds (if they are bonds) of his spare and rhythmic prose and creates something which, in imaginative power, takes its place beside poetic drama. No writer of our time has so magnificently harnessed thought to imagination."

It is a detached view of life, but consistent to its own metaphysical plane. As such it opened up entirely new paths in the theatre which no other dramatist in the world has dared to pursue or expand. *Back to Methuselah*, hardly playable in one evening and usually spread over three, remains unique and a law unto itself.

It solidified also the bonds Shaw was to create in the next two decades with certain actors and actresses, who became known as gifted exponents of his later plays in the way that Barker and Lillah McCarthy and Mrs. Patrick Campbell were known in the case of the earlier ones. It is one of Shaw's good fortunes that he outlived generations of good actors and theatre managements, only to find others equally talented to replace them (it is the eternally wonderful basis of Eve's speech on Nature's planning of human genius, so that each generation contains its approximately constant quota of poet and artist and musician). Hesione and the Serpent, as later Orinthia in *The Apple Cart*, were characters based in part on Mrs. Patrick Campbell ("Mrs. Hesione Hushabye in *Heartbreak House*, the Serpent in *Methuselah*, whom I always hear speaking with your voice, and Orinthia: all you, to say nothing of Eliza, who was only a joke," wrote Shaw to her in 1929). But through age or other causes she never played any of them, and they were all to become famous in England in the portrayals of Edith Evans, a great later actress whose wit, style and silken-silver voice made her a supreme interpreter of Shaw no less than of the Restoration dramatists.

The Eve to Dame Edith's Serpent at Birmingham was Gwen Ffrangcon-Davies, another actress of unusual quality; the Reverend William Haslam, three-hundred-year-old Archbishop of York and He-Ancient (to Edith Evans' She-Ancient) Cedric Hardwicke, whose association with Shaw as a "star" player was to continue in many notable parts into the thirties;[2] and Sir Barry Jackson himself was to become above all others the manager most responsible for the staging of Shaw's later plays, not only in Birmingham and London but from 1929 until 1939 at the annual Malvern Festival, which became for three weeks each August a cultural center of which Shaw was the acknowledged master dramatist.

Back to Methuselah by its very length and nature could not be a commercial success, as Shaw realized. In an amusing account of Barry Jackson's first approaching him, during a performance at the Birmingham Repertory Theatre to which someone had taken Shaw, he wrote years later:

> I had never heard of Barry Jackson, and possibly betrayed that fact unguardedly. I found out afterwards that he had been producing my plays for years, in some cases giving the first performance, only to see that distinction ascribed to others in my published records. My Secretary had arranged all these exploits as a matter of routine without calling my attention to them.
>
> I felt my way cautiously, gathering that he had built the theatre and owned it, until he said that he wanted to produce *Methuselah*. I asked him was he mad. He intimated that though not sane enough to keep out of theatre management he could manage more or less lucidly. I demanded further whether he

[2] "If I emerged as an actor of any stature at all, I owe it to my association with Bernard Shaw," Sir Cedric maintains in his autobiography, *A Victorian in Orbit* (Methuen, London, 1962).

wished his wife and children to die in the workhouse. He replied that he was not married.

Nevertheless, the next important play of Shaw's did not need the ministrations of an unusually bold and eccentric provincial manager. It was *Saint Joan*, considered by many his masterpiece, and in spite of some initial peculiarly blunt and shortsighted criticisms by the drama critics of New York and London, a play that has held its own and even increased its reputation on the stages of the world for nearly forty years.

It was Charlotte who first introduced to Shaw the idea of writing a play on Joan of Arc, but in spite of the literature, including the trial records (which unlike many medieval historical documents have been fully preserved in France), that she put in his way to read, he did not at first show great interest. He told Sybil Thorndike that it was only after seeing her performance as Beatrice Cenci, in a private theatre club production of Shelley's long-banned play *The Cenci*, that he really felt the incentive to write the play on Joan, for he realized at once she was the actress he needed for the part.

He then wrote it with great speed ("I did not write *Saint Joan*: she took the pen out of my hand," he said afterwards); only to find that Laurence Binyon, the playwright and poet, had also just completed a play on Joan without knowing that Shaw was writing one. "I warned off Masefield, I warned off Drinkwater, but I forgot Binyon," commented Shaw ruefully. Sybil Thorndike had been approached to play the Binyon Joan, and Lewis Casson, her husband, ventured to write to Shaw to ask if he had continued with his own project and still wanted Sybil to play in it. He wrote back as we have seen, adding "Of course Sybil plays my Joan. Let ——— play Binyon's." The matter, however, was settled by Binyon's generously and modestly withdrawing his play when he heard that Shaw had written one on the same subject, for he recognized his could not compete.

In fact, *Saint Joan*, like many Shaw plays during this period, had its first production in New York, so Sybil Thorndike did not 'create' the part, which was played first in America by Winifred Lenihan, in a production by the Theatre Guild at the Garrick Theatre on December 28, 1923. Its English premiere, under the joint management of Mary Moore and Sybil Thorndike, was at the New Theatre, London, on March 26, 1924. Both productions ran for well over 200 performances, and Sybil Thorndike herself toured in the play extensively and acted in a number of revivals, in the last of which, seven years later, I saw her at the Theatre Royal, Brighton, when I was still in my teens.

Many fine actresses have played Joan since, including several at the Old Vic,[3] the distinguished American actress Katherine Cornell, the Irish actress Siobhan McKenna, and Sybil Thorndike's own daughter, Ann Casson, who to my mind came nearest in style, interpretation and voice to her mother, though in fact they deliberately avoided discussing the part before Ann's performance took place. It was not, though, entirely by chance that the similarity of voice should seem to me, across a gap of some fifteen years, so striking; the timbre of the voices is by nature and heredity very close, and Sybil Thorndike later told me that one of her most vivid memories of Shaw at rehearsal was the inflection of his voice when demonstrating Joan's speeches to her—an inflection and emphasis of words she repeated, as far as she could, in performance. As a result, when she herself hears another actress in the part many of the speeches sound to her odd, for she cannot help hearing them still as Shaw spoke them and desired her to

[3] The latest of these, Barbara Jefford, is appearing in the part with an Old Vic company in the United States as I write this.

speak them. This interested me because, as I told her, whenever I read the play it is always *her* voice I hear, with its individual ring and interpretation, in Joan's speeches, and no other actress has ever succeeded in obliterating this first impression, even though I was so young at the time.

In Sybil Thorndike, in fact, Shaw found as he realized his ideal interpreter, able by character and art to cover both aspects he needed in his Joan: the religious mystic and the commonsensical country woman and born general. In this actress, a religious woman (she was the daughter of a canon of Rochester Cathedral) and a generous and active fighter for social causes who had been something of a tomboy in youth, all aspects of Joan fused in a way that has never completely been repeated since, for she acted not only under Shaw's personal direction but from the inward conviction of natural temperament and personal belief.

Her "Light your fire!," withdrawing the recantation, had the ring of genuine religious transportation in defiance; her speech in Rouen Cathedral on loneliness had, too, this sense of transfiguration as well as unutterable pathos in isolation; her country girl's simple yet transcendent faith shone through the practical urgency of her pleading for horse and armor; and throughout her passages with courtiers and churchmen, with Dunois the soldier and the weak, vacillating, but not unshrewd and wasp-tongued Dauphin, one was conscious without question of a girl with the physical resources of a born soldier and campaigner, plus the mental qualities that make for the strategist and general of original genius. Her mind struck fire out of the play, like metal against a tinder; and the fire was not only the saint's fire but the burning zeal of a human being a little in love—as Dunois says of her—with war. A picture of Joan without either facet—the mystic and the soldier—can never be a true one.

She insists that Shaw was fundamentally a religious

man, and that this is proved by his long friendship with and many letters to Dame Laurentia McLachlan, the Abbess of the Benedictines of Stanbrook Abbey, with whom the actress has talked much of Shaw since his death. Always observant, he had noticed the wide eyes of mystics in pictures and told her at rehearsal: "Keep your eyes wide open—wider than natural." In such acting details they built up a portrait valid and expressive on the stage no less than the printed page.

In fact, the association in *Saint Joan* that was of so much importance to them both was a justification of Shaw's own insight into the elements that go to make an actress. When he had first seen Sybil Thorndike at an audition very early in her career, he had said to her brusquely but not unkindly in effect: "Go away for four years, have children, learn about life, and then come back to the stage and act." Applying to understudy one of Shaw's favorite actresses in his plays—the beautiful speaker (he set great store by dramatic speech) Ellen O'Malley—as Candida, she had overacted with all the enthusiasm of youth, indiscipline and her own native vitality. Soon afterwards she met and married Lewis Casson and did, as it happens, much what Shaw had advised. But Shaw, she later learned, had also said to someone in the theatre at the time: "Watch her"; for he sensed the natural talent in this girl who at twenty-three years of age was young for her years, emotionally and in looks, and greatly inexperienced in life (she thinks this youthfulness a natural characteristic that runs in families—Shaw had it; she herself preserves it as an active actress of eighty, and watches it now in her own grandchildren).

Years later, in 1920, she and her husband asked Shaw's permission to produce *Candida* at the Holborn Empire in London, where they were also presenting under their own management a season of Greek tragedy that placed Sybil Thorndike at the pinnacle of the English theatre as a tragedienne. Shaw attended rehearsals, which were held in the afternoon as he was spending his mornings rehearsing Mrs. Pat in a revival of *Pygmalion.* They recall how pale and exhausted he seemed on arrival. The intolerable strains of the attachment to Mrs. Pat (about whose performances, even at the height of his infatuation, he never minced words of criticism, which she was sometimes wise enough to heed) seem still to have weighed on him seven years after the affair's brief, fierce blaze of riot. One doubts if the tiredness was purely physical, the result of professional wrangling, but not also an exhaustion of spirit from the re-emergence of fires dimmed by time, but not yet quite spent.

It would be difficult to imagine two great actresses more unlike in temperament than Dame Sybil Thorndike and Mrs. Patrick Campbell, but in one sense Sybil Thorndike had the same technical problem with Joan that her predecessor had with Eliza: she was forty-one years of age when she first played the part of this girl of nineteen, and her natural youthfulness of spirit and appearance was certainly needed. With her short, straight golden hair and strong face with its surprisingly delicate profile, she conveyed this youthfulness, even seven years later when I saw her; for Joan's was a tough youthfulness, mature in vision, and as Shaw pointed out she was no romantic heroine as popular cartoon (it is no more) and some misguided and too glamorous actresses have made her. "To the more romantic spectators, I must break the news that though Joan inspired strong likes and dislikes, and was not at all bad looking, she had no love affairs. There is overwhelming testimony that her complete neutrality in this respect was accepted as evidence of her divine mission by her soldier comrades."

The greatness of the play itself now hardly needs exposition. It is great not only in its many-sided, imaginative yet intensely living portrait of Joan but in the element most disliked and misunderstood by some of its earlier critics (still hidebound, one supposes, to Victorian ideas of the function of the theatre). This was above all its quality of putting the historical scene in focus in time; in presenting vividly not only the martyrdom of a unique personality but in dramatically analyzing the political and ecclesiastical forces that set themselves, from infelt necessity, to crush her.

To do this Shaw went with an historian's integrity to the actual historical sources; but transformed them into play material which was also material for discussion on medieval ideas illuminated by modern experience, looking into the past. "We must face the fact," he wrote, "that society is founded on intolerance," and that this is "quite as characteristic of our own age as of the Middle Ages."

> I write in full view of the Middle ages . . . it is the business of the stage to make its figures more intelligible to themselves than they would be in real life; for by no other means can they be made intelligible to the audience. And in this case Cauchon and Lemaître[4] have to make intelligible not only themselves but the Church and the Inquisition, just as Warwick has to make the feudal system intelligible, the three between them having thus to make a twentieth-century audience conscious of an epoch fundamentally different from its own. Obviously the real Cauchon, Lemaître, and Warwick could not have done this: they were part of the Middle Ages themselves, and therefore as unconscious of its peculiarities as of the atomic formula of the air they breathed . . . All I can claim is that. . . . as far as I can gather from the available documentation, and from such powers of divination as I possess, the things I represent these three exponents of the drama as saying are the things they actually would have said if they had known what they were really doing. And beyond this neither drama nor history can go in my hands.

For dramatic purposes he telescoped the characters of

[4] The Inquisitor.

Dunois and the Duc D'Alençon, young men who fought with Joan and apparently sufficiently similar in character as far as history's rather meager records allow one to deduce; and de Stogumber does not escape parody, though moving in his final mad and gentle appearance in the Epilogue (lack of imagination in cruelty is one of Shaw's most piercing, and basically compassionate, themes). But one is not conscious in performance of distortion but of a penetration below the surface of events which by some magic rivets the audience in a way political argument and long speeches (and the Inquisitor's takes several minutes to deliver) could not possibly have been expected to have done before this play took the stage. Shaw's method with history is accepted now and has been followed in other modern historical plays, though nowhere with such magnificence of vision and intellect. His influence in this respect can be seen in Anouilh's *The Lark*, a technically different drama of Joan based on the same historical records, but with a Warwick quite obviously deriving from Shaw's ironic spokesman for the feudal barons, which had little to do with the statesman Richard Beauchamp, Earl of Warwick, who took part, it is true, in the French wars but was mainly notable for his wise but perhaps too religious guidance as tutor of the boy King Henry VI. Shaw, of course, does not make Anouilh's mistake of describing this Earl of Warwick as "Warwick the Kingmaker," who was a Neville by birth and succeeded to the title through marriage a generation later (less forgivably, the makers of the film of Shaw's play, in which Sir John Gielgud played Warwick, did so!).

The Epilogue, showing Joan's rehabilitation by the Church which condemned her within living memory of her, has always been harshly criticized by some for levity; but as Shaw wrote: "I could hardly be expected to stultify myself by implying that Joan's history in the world ended unhappily with her execution, instead of beginning there.

It was necessary by hook or crook to shew the canonized Joan as well as the incinerated one; for many a woman has got herself burnt by carelessly whisking a muslin skirt into the drawing-room fireplace, but getting canonized is a different matter, and a more important one. So I am afraid the epilogue must stand."

It stands, in spite of flaws (the unconquerable jester in Shaw), through its wonderful litany to Joan by those who condemned and supported her; through her own bright undimmed spirit and final cry that pierces the heart: "O God that madest this beautiful earth, when will it be ready to receive Thy saints? How long, O Lord, how long?" It was Sybil Thorndike's most moving moment, and one that no one who heard or saw her ever can forget.

The directors of the London production were Shaw himself and Lewis Casson (who also played de Stogumber), and Raymond Massey as La Hire and Jack Hawkins (still at drama school) as Dunois' page are names on the program (like Morris Carnovsky, La Hire in New York) recognizable now as of future eminence. Ernest Thesiger, the original London Dauphin, was to have a long association with Shaw's plays as an actor. In the thirties, the part was brilliantly played by Maurice Evans at the Old Vic, and later by the same actor with Katherine Cornell in America. The London designer was Charles Ricketts, a Royal Academy artist of imaginative stage gifts, and his striking costumes glowed against the simplicity and beauty of his settings. A few years later he also designed notable settings and costumes for D'Oyly Carte Opera productions of *The Mikado* and *The Gondoliers*: the only time in England until the release of the Gilbert and Sullivan operas from copyright that they could be said to attain real visual distinction.

The morning after the London first night, Sybil Thorndike saw Shaw striding across Leicester Square, his ulster flapping like an agitated bird on wing. "What shall we write next?" he said, pausing, as it were, in full flight. She suggested a play on Queen Elizabeth or Richard III. "Too successful," was his verdict on the characters. Joan's failure made her stuff for tragedy, as he knew; of such is drama born. Nevertheless, it is a pity he never tackled Elizabeth, a great woman of contradictory impulses no dramatist has ever captured significantly on the stage (I am not forgetting Schiller). And Richard, now we know more of his true character and the mystery of his reign, might have been a challenging subject for this breaker-down of historians' myths and traditions.

He was genius enough himself not to be above contradictory impulses. Sir Barry Jackson, years later, suggested Bonnie Prince Charlie to him as a subject, only to be met with its rejection on the grounds that he could not write about failures! But by then Shaw was old, his powers tiring, and he knew it; perhaps any excuse that came to mind would do. Failure and success in great lives is in any case highly relative, according to the point of view.

Saint Joan is indisputably greater than any play he wrote afterwards, although *In Good King Charles's Golden Days*, first produced in the last prewar Malvern Festival in 1939, must rank among the best of his plays in style and quality of thought, and something of a miracle—like Verdi's *Falstaff*—for an octogenarian creator. *The Apple Cart*, the first play at the first Malvern Festival on August 19, 1929, was however a sparkling lampoon on the Labour Party in government that has scintillated not less brightly in the postwar London revivals, one at the Arts Theatre with Jack Hawkins in the brilliant role of King Magnus, and some years later at the Haymarket Theatre with Noel Coward as Magnus and Margaret Leighton as his mistress Orinthia in the important Interlude.

This comedy had the rare distinction of being first presented in Polish at the Teatr Polski in Warsaw! Its English production was by Sir Barry Jackson's management, the four performances at Malvern being followed by a very long run with the same cast at the Queen's Theatre in London, with Cedric Hardwicke as King Magnus and Edith Evans as Orinthia.

Orinthia was based on Mrs. Patrick Campbell, who at first without an inkling of the fact angled for Shaw to read her the play (she herself at the time was rehearsing and playing a fine part of an elderly Jewess in *The Matriarch*, based on G. B. Stern's novel—her last West End triumph as an actress). He proved suspiciously coy about doing so, though it is true the rehearsals and production of a revival of *Major Barbara*, with Sybil Thorndike, as well as arrangements to travel abroad, created many demands on his time. Then a friend blew the gaffe to Mrs. Campbell: Orinthia was the King's mistress, or something suspiciously verging on it, with a suite in Buckingham Palace supplied by the Civil List; and she wishes to be Queen of England, while he refuses on the grounds that he does not want to hurt his wife Jemima. "I asked him why he did not get you to play it—and he said 'no one could play themselves.' "

"I don't know why you feel shy—the scene isn't true, though it may amuse you to fancy it so," wrote Mrs. Pat to him with rather ominous calmness; and begged once again that he should come and read it to her, with an incidental sinister query of his legal right to put her in a play without her permission.

"I ran away from you at Sandwich because I wanted to remain Queen of the Kingdom of my heart—but I suppose you mustn't humble the King in your play like that—"

This outrageously flamboyant interpretation of the past (ending quaintly with the prosaic postscript: "Do look out for the change in the weather") stunned Shaw into something like acquiescence. "Of course the scene isn't true; but you will recognize bits and scraps of it. And there are perhaps gleams of truth in it here and there. Which of us knows the whole truth? Not I." But he added hastily: "But I can't read it to you now because I do not possess a copy," an assurance he found himself forced to repeat as urgent request followed urgent request, mixed inextricably with "Dearest Joeys" and talk about "illegal acts" (often in the same breath of the pen) and still more hints about the large sums his letters to her would fetch in America ("I would like them published they are so lovely—one in particular should be placed between two leaves of gold"; a statement which doubtless caused him —racking his memory—some alarm and despondency). He stuck by his decision not to let her publish, and proved immune to such warnings as "Don't go to your grave dearest regretting I didn't play in your *Apple cart*" and "Malvern for a week in August will suit me. I have friends living there who will put me up."

"*The Apple Cart* will be safer with Edith Evans; and the King will have a fair chance instead of being upset and unhinged," he replied from the safe distance of Dubrovnik, adding recklessly: "However, bewitch Barry Jackson if you can." But that her capacity in that direction still echoed from the past, and was not wholly spent on him even now, is shown in a note of baffled exasperation and query: "I have seen no notices of the play[5] (being cut off from the papers here) and you tell me not a word of it except that you despised the producer. I daresay you told him so. But what happened? Is the play a success? It might so easily be with you in it— if you would let it, whatever it may be."

It was unfortunate he allowed himself the luxury of quoting Oscar Wilde ("For all blackmail the men they love") in his next letter, for *her* next proclaimed she had been to a ball "and met Miss Edith Evans, who gazed

[5] *The Matriarch.*

eagerly at me saying she was playing *me* in *The Apple Cart* at Malvern and in Birmingham and London." And the fat was indeed in the fire! "There is of course nothing that could give any clue to the public—above all to the Press. It can be a secret between us," he wrote soothingly. "How can it be a 'secret' between us—when Edith Evans told me she was playing *me*?" she screamed back in wrath, and one can see her point, though he countered with "Edith Evans guessed of course" and an assurance that "perhaps half a dozen others know" that does not carry conviction.

She was genuinely hurt, and he knew it, and rewrote some lines (she still hadn't read the play) to put the Orinthia-King Magnus relationship somewhere nearer a kind of fairyland where only—as Magnus states—she could be his queen. "Does that cure the soreness at your heart?" he wrote hopefully, only to be drowned in her tears at his letting Orinthia run down Magnus' wife (Charlotte, in her mind, as of course *au fond* in his). "My love for you was the love of a child who feels safe," she moaned: a surprising interpretation of her flight from Sandwich, at which he began to lose his temper, and she in turn to talk of lawyers and imperiously demand: "Tear it up, and rewrite it with every scrap of the mischievous vulgarian omitted, and all suburban backchat against Charlotte and suggested harlotry against me, and the inference of your own superiority wiped out."

"I don't feel it to be wrong," scribbled Shaw on her letter. "It plays magnificently. Orinthia never loses her distinction and beauty even when she rolls on the floor. If she did I would amputate her without a moment's hesitation, and be ashamed of her. But I'm not . . . Besides, Orinthia is not a portrait: she is a study for which you sat as a model in bits only—though the magnificence of the picture is due to you."

Separately, and briefly, he wrote:

Dearest

You are such a fool! Oh, such a, *such* a, SUCH a fool!

Goodnight,

G.B.S.

It was not unaffectionate, and though she clamored some more the end of the matter on his side. He was right; it played magnificently (partly, no doubt, owing to the superb gifts of the players and Edith Evans' own personal magic, as vital in its way as Mrs. Pat's). And it was, after all, in spite of all the fuss, only an interlude, and glimpse into Magnus' private life, joining two long acts of urbane political battle between the King and his government. He included for Magnus the excessively long speech now to be associated with one character or another in most plays by Shaw, and its beautiful cogency (and Hardwicke's reputed equal cogency and style in its delivery) held the audience no less than the verbal fireworks and amusing satire elsewhere. The play, high comedy in style for all its socialist parody (there were political portraits in it no less derivative than Orinthia), was not without its serious undercurrents and one genuinely moving outburst: by the frustrated, serious-minded Powermistress-General, Lysistrata, who was played by Eileen Beldon, a fine actress who had been in *Back to Methuselah* at Birmingham and was to have a long association with Shaw plays.

Its final quip of fantasy, when the American Ambassador to London generously brings a United States offer to return to the Commonwealth, has always gone particularly well with audiences on both sides of the Atlantic. The historical interest of the scene is more in the original London player of the part: that James Carew who as a young actor had been so flatteringly scooped up by Ellen Terry, during the rehearsals of *Captain Brassbound's Conversion*, over twenty years before.

The next new play by Shaw at the Malvern Festival was *Too True To Be Good*. It had first been presented by the

Theatre Guild in New York early in 1932 and in September was given at the New Theatre, London, where it dismayed the critics and ran for only six weeks. It is mainly remembered as the play in which Shaw achieved some entertaining comedy by putting his friend T. E. Lawrence (Lawrence of Arabia) on the stage under the name of Private Meek, a *nom de guerre* deriving from Lawrence's habit of resigning commissions after the War and taking service in the Royal Air Force and the Tank Corps under the names of Ross and Shaw. (Shaw, under which name he served almost to his death, was of course borrowed from G.B.S.)

A later play, *Ross*, by Terence Rattigan, dealing with Lawrence's first postwar service as an aircraftsman, might be said to be a counterbalance to Shaw's picture, for apart from one scene of delicious irony (the scene with Allenby) its emphasis is wholly serious and psychological, exploring Lawrence's inner uncertainties so much at the expense of every other facet (including the Elizabethan high adventurer out of his time) that he emerges as a strangely glum character, moving but curiously lacking in the force and impetus, the sense of comedy, the many-sidedness of an enigmatic yet always zestful and vibrant personality.

Lawrence's wide archaeological knowledge, love of music, and passion to achieve literary distinction, are equally ignored by Shaw; but his small, tough, secretly amused private, taking command in a desert place over everything from stores and interpreting to parleys with local chieftains and actual tactics; staggering his superior officer not only by his calm resource but the roar of his motorcycle driven across mountain roads at eighty miles an hour; really gives a better picture, for all its comedy slant, of the basic quality of Lawrence's character and achievement. Somewhere between the two plays, but nearer to Shaw's, lies the whole Lawrence; but Lawrence was alive when Shaw wrote, and obviously there had to be certain repressions. Lawrence indeed enjoyed the play thoroughly—writing an appreciative letter to Walter Hudd, the actor of Meek, after he had slipped unobtrusively and unrecognized into a performance at Birmingham. Oddly, the two later sat shyly glancing at each other across the tables of a nearby canteen. Hudd was chosen partly for his striking resemblance to Lawrence (he was also a first-rate actor, who had played the Dauphin brilliantly in Sybil Thorndike's last tour of *Saint Joan*), and his performance, meticulously and militarily correct yet always on the verge, as it were, of a smile, was one of the genuine successes of the play. Shaw himself he found helpful and generously ready to listen to a young actor's problems during a long walk on which they found themselves together.

Shaw had first met Lawrence in 1922, when Sir Sidney Cockerell, Director of the Fitzwilliam Museum, Cambridge, and a former secretary to William Morris and the Kelmscott Press, brought him to the Shaws' flat in Adelphi Terrace to help carry away one of the Augustus John portraits of Shaw, which Shaw had given to the Museum. It was the beginning of a long friendship, during which Shaw acted frequently as critic of Lawrence's MSS, which he punctuated himself. Later he was a welcome visitor at Lawrence's cottage, Clouds Hill, in Dorset, used by Lawrence as a refuge from the R.A.F. camp nearby. ("He came in," said Lawrence of Shaw's first visit, for which he had excitedly and carefully prepared, "sniffing the air and taking stock of everything like a sergeant-major. I really think he liked it.") It was Lawrence who in Dorset also, with some misgiving, introduced the Shaws to Thomas Hardy and his wife: a meeting which proved unexpectedly successful or—as Lawrence put it—"a gorgeous mixture."

It is easy to understand the mutual appeal of the two men. In some ways, indeed, Lawrence could have been Shaw's son, and Charlotte certainly sensed the likeness and became devoted to the younger man, encouraging his literary ambitions with warm enthusiasm. Lawrence had an innate fear of women as a rule, and though he was certainly not a homosexual, as some have suggested, his monasticism and sexual repressions (he had a typical hatred of being touched) were intensified by a self-imposed spiritual discipline and life of hardihood to which Shaw, himself abstemious in sex and preaching far greater necessities in human life and mind, instinctively responded. They were mentally and spiritually in tune, sharing many of the same artistic pleasures and tastes. The irony of their wit matched, and tended to play over the same objects. And it is possibly true that in both the perennial youthfulness, the "Joey" instinct to clown and cock a snook at convention and authority, even the withdrawal from sex—complete in Lawrence's case, partial for at least the major part of Shaw's life—were aspects of a kind of emotional immaturity. In some ways neither man ever quite grew up, and significantly the name Peter Pan has been used by different observers to describe both.

Shaw himself was certainly not unaware of the resemblance when he wrote of him:[6]

> With the single doubtful exception of myself, no man of our time has had such a power of tempting journalists and even diplomatists to tell lies about him as Lawrence. Look at the obituary notices! They are all headed "Mystery Man." Yet there has never been any mystery about Lawrence since the end of the War. He changed his name twice; but everybody knew it as well as when the King changed his name from Guelph to Windsor . . . When he was in the middle of the stage with ten limelights blazing on him, everybody pointed to him and said: "See! He is in hiding. He hates publicity." He was so conspicuous that he was bothered by it and really did make some half-hearted efforts to hide him-

[6] *T. E. Lawrence by his Friends*, a symposium edited by A. W. Lawrence, Cape, London, 1937.

self; but it was no use: he was the most impish of comedians, and always did something that turned up the lights again.

Shaw's admiration was nevertheless genuine and equally given to Lawrence's *Seven Pillars of Wisdom*, which he described as a "masterpiece." And he had a profound respect for and understanding both of Lawrence's refusal to make money out of the blood of the Arabs he had fought with (the *Seven Pillars* was issued in costly, individually printed copies, along Morris lines, under subscription) and of the "highly sensitive and imaginative man" who had inevitable scruples of conscience after killing Turks—as Lawrence, unlike most commanders, was forced to do—personally and in cold blood. He did not, and could not in Lawrence's lifetime, relance such sensitive wounds of soul in his own comedy; but those who imagine Shaw was therefore unaware of or indifferent to them understand neither Shaw the man nor Shaw the writer of anything but plays. Like Lawrence, he himself hid such things behind a mask that needed to be all the steelier for the compassion and hatred of suffering beneath it.

Too True To Be Good, labeled a "Political Extravaganza," falls into two parts. The first is a fantastical comedy about a young lady hypochondriac who is whisked off to enjoy life and her natural health by a chaplain-turned-burglar, under the nose of a languishing Germ or Monster who complains bitterly that though he is blamed as the germ that gave her the measles, the real truth of the matter is that *she* has given the measles to *him*. It is closed by this not unendearing creature's categorical warning: "The play is now virtually over; but the characters will discuss it at great length for two acts more. The exit doors are all in order. Goodnight."

The second part carries out this warning. The characters in search of sun have all turned up in mountainous bandit country somewhere in the Middle East, and are supplemented for good argument by the British Army (represented by Private Meek, his water-colorist colonel, and a Sergeant fond of women but also of reading Bunyan and the Bible), and by an Elder who turns out to be the Burglar's father, an atheist who thunders his lost faith in rationalism like some disillusioned prophet from the mouth of a cave.

In craftsmanship and design the play is cracked down the middle; and for the first time we become too painfully aware of the way the clown in Shaw is taking a descending slant with advancing age (he was now well over seventy). The wit of the dialogue is cheapened by jokes at which a Planché would not have turned up his nose. Yet rereading it today, some of its great speeches come like "the iron lightning" (one of Shaw's finer phrases) of revelation. It is prophetic in a way more illuminating now than then: its whole theme being the disillusionments and cracked and changing moral standards of a generation that has gone through the fire of modern war. The effects of that kind of war are more vivid in the light of today's "wind of change" than in the still uncertain light of the early thirties, when the Bright Young Things had settled down into semirespectability and the shadow of Hitler had hardly begun to lengthen across Europe.

"Look at these two books," says the Sergeant of the Bible and *The Pilgrim's Progress*. "I used to believe every word of them because they seemed to have nothing to do with real life. But war brought those old stories home quite real; and then one starts asking questions. Look at this bit here [he points to a page of *The Pilgrim's Progress*]. It's on the very first page of it. 'I am for certain informed that this our city will be burned with fire from heaven, in which fearful overthrow both myself, with thee my wife, and you my sweet babes, shall miserably come to ruin, except some way of escape can be found whereby we may be delivered.' Well, London and Paris and Berlin and

Rome and the rest of them will be burned with fire from heaven all right in the next war; thats certain. Theyre all Cities of Destruction. And our Government chaps are running about with a great burden of corpses and debts on their backs, crying 'What must we do to be saved?' There it is: not a story in a book as it used to be, but God's truth in the real actual world. And all the comfort they get is 'Flee from the wrath to come.' But where are they to flee to? . . . The man in the book says 'Do you see yonder shining light?' Well, today the place is blazing with shining lights: shining lights in parliament, in the papers, in the churches, and in the books that they call Outlines—Outlines of History and Science and what not—and in spite of all their bally-hoo here we are waiting in the City of Destruction like so many sheep for the wrath to come."

The Patient has run away and thrown off the burden of a self-sacrificing but overwhelming mother; because in Shaw's philosophy, as in Christ's, family relationships are not as important as individual freedom to follow a creed or simply find liberty from a lie. And the mother's coddling was a lie, mere slavery to a convention, bringing happiness and real love neither to herself nor the girl. They can live together again only on a basis of mutual freedom, ignoring the accidental relationship of birth. This shocked many at the time more even than Shaw's mocking at the sanctity of Empire-building and the Army, for 'The Family' is a bastion of English moral convention, in spite of the many unhappy, ill-assorted, squabbling and misunderstanding bunches of people linked under that name for whom the only sensible thing is parting, so that they can realize their individual characters and gifts without restraint. The animals know this, pushing out the young ones to fend for themselves once they have attained adult status; and they don't try to keep the claws in after departure, being unlike humans unpossessive in this sense. Many relations are happy and well adjusted to each other, respecting each other's individualities and points of view; more are not, especially in comparison with deeper friendships outside the family circle. Yet we still haven't broken down the general pretense, in spite of recognizing it as the cause of much juvenile delinquency; although Shaw's moral in *Too True To Be Good* would probably be more widely accepted if the play were produced today.

Indeed, it should be given a new hearing; for Shaw was a prophet always some thirty years ahead of his time, and the wind of change has blown down more conventional edifices since the Second World War than the First. We are nearer, now, to his characters because after two wars more ready to admit his truths. Then, he wrote for some, the intellectual few in the main; now, for our society as a whole. The Elder is no longer solitary in his bewilderment:

> . . . the universe of Isaac Newton, which has been an impregnable citadel of modern civilization for three hundred years, has crumbled like the walls of Jericho before the criticism of Einstein . . . Everything was calculable; everything happened because it must . . . And now—now—what is left of it? The orbit of the electron obeys no law: it chooses one path and rejects another: it is as capricious as the planet Mercury, who wanders from his road to warm his hands at the sun. All is caprice: the calculable world has become incalculable: Purpose and Design, the pretexts for all the vilest superstitions, have risen from the dead to cast down the mighty from their seats and put paper crowns on presumptuous fools.

And his son, the priest-burglar, ends the play in a speech of three columns that is like an apostrophe to the sixties:

> But how are we to bear this dreadful new nakedness: the nakedness of the souls who until now have always disguised themselves from one another in beautiful impossible idealisms to enable them to bear one another's company. The iron lightning of war has burnt great rents in these angelic veils,

just as it has smashed great holes in our cathedral roofs and torn great gashes in our hillsides. Our souls go in rags now; and the young are spying through the holes and getting glimpses of the reality that was hidden. And they are not horrified; they exult in having found us out; they expose their own souls; and when we their elders desperately try to patch our torn clothes with scraps of the old material, the young lay violent hands on us and tear from us even the rags that were left to us. . . .

Nature never intended me for soldiering or thieving: I am by nature and destiny a preacher. I am the new Ecclesiastes. But I have no Bible, no creed: the war has shot both out of my hands . . . we have outgrown our religion, outgrown our political system, outgrown our own strength of mind and character. . . .

It is a play for the Royal Court Theatre of our own time, half a century after Shaw in middle age first entered it and broke down the barriers of theatre illusion. It gives voice to a generation of playwrights with plenty of ammunition, but insufficient vocal or mental guns with which to fire it. They have reduced mankind's plight to fit within the narrow walls of a kitchen; what is wanted now is a new Shaw to blast the walls and fire the ammunition across the wider wasteland of mind and society as a whole. And failing a new Shaw, the old one has power in his lungs yet.

The splendid rhetoric of this play was finely discharged by Ralph Richardson as the Sergeant and Cedric Hardwicke as the Burglar. On tour after the London run, the Burglar was superbly played by Donald Wolfit, a young actor then hardly known, and the Patient by a lively young redhead completely unheard of, named Greer Garson. Shaw's plays have seen the rise of almost as many outstanding players as Shakespeare's; his prose demands resources of voice and intellect, diction and rhythm, which only the highly intelligent and professional actor can muster.

Another political play along the lines of *The Apple*

Cart, On the Rocks, was produced in 1933 but its run was short and it is memorable now mainly for Shaw's pert quip: "The only man who ever really understood Parliament was old Guy Fawkes." *The Simpleton of the Unexpected Isles,* a return to the Creative Evolution theme of *Back to Methuselah* but with an Eastern mystic twist, did not reach London from Malvern until after the War, at the Arts Theatre, though it was played in New York. A short "comediettina for two voices," *Village Wooing*, was more successful. Sybil Thorndike played the leading part, a young woman on a sea cruise and subsequently serving behind the counter in a country grocery store, at the Little Theatre in 1934 (Shaw carefully corrected her Cockney accent at rehearsal to one nearer Wiltshire, just as he had insisted on Joan's speaking with a North Country accent, in the idiom in which he had written the part). The character of the literary "man pursued" was obviously based on Shaw himself. It is an unimportant but entertaining piece that has been revived a surprising number of times, including on British television some twenty-six years after it was written.

Another comedy, *The Millionairess*, in which Edith Evans toured before the War, was accounted one of Shaw's failures until it took the London stage, in a very delayed-action debut, at the New Theatre in 1952, with Katharine Hepburn as the aggressively vital millionairess Epifania and Robert Helpmann as the Egyptian doctor. This unexpected success was followed even more unexpectedly by a film version, with Sophia Loren (no less) and Peter Sellers in the two leading roles. A "Vitalist" (as Shaw once described himself) tends always to take an audience by the throat and shake it into submission, and this Katharine Hepburn did with the play. Shaw's heroine has plenty of guts and business ability, and wins her man by proving it; but the play reads badly for Shaw and its "sweat shop" scene was an anachronism even in 1935, when it was written.

Two plays from Malvern stand out in a sudden revival of Shaw's comic sweep and mental alertness. *Geneva* he grew to hate. "*Geneva* is a horrible play," he wrote to Mrs. Pat in December, 1938, when it was enjoying a highly successful London run. "I went to see it the other day and it made me quite ill. Splendid for the actors though. The performances are like election meetings."

In the light of later events its parody of Hitler (Battler) and Mussolini (Bombardone) can be painful to the oversensitive; but it cannot really be dismissed so lightly and its satire is the more telling for the fact that (as always with Shaw) both sides get some reasonable if specious argument on their side. The setting was the Court of International Justice at the Hague, and the more humane and serious political undercurrents and national responsibilities were certainly not ignored. The Judge, a wise and brilliant barrister-figure, was successively played, very finely and with a great sense of mental power in reserve, by Alexander Knox and Donald Wolfit. Hudd was the hysterical Battler (in Lohengrin costume) and the always superb and incisive Shavian actor, Cecil Trouncer, made a strongly Caesarian opposite as Bombardone, here (and perhaps historically) the more effectual reasoner. Ernest Thesiger also shone in the silken Chamberlain diplomacy—hand of steel in velvet glove—of the British minister, Sir Orpheus Midlander. As Shaw said, it was "splendid for the actors," and their vigorous or subtle sense of fun helped the play to achieve an astonishingly long run of 237 performances.

It was a resurge of Shavian vigor that reached a higher peak in *In Good King Charles's Golden Days* at Malvern in 1939, the following year. Produced during a golden August, just before the outbreak of war, it had a mature serenity in which the fun sprang always from wit and character. King Charles II (a statesman Shaw abundantly admired), Isaac Newton, George Fox, founder of the Society of Friends, known as the Quakers, Kneller the painter, are brought together in unlikely historical circumstances but not impossibly in point of period, and used engagingly to set spinning a scintillating and often illuminating discussion of the nature of politics, science, religion and art. It is true to do this adequately Shaw had to give Kneller, an inferior mind, some of Hogarth's intelligence, including the greater painter's dictum that "the line of beauty is a curve"—an instinctive artistic insight which shatters Newton's careful mathematical theories a century or two before Einstein. But all the other characters were strictly contemporary and representative of a wonderful flowering of thought and art, as Shaw realized.

"Now anyone who considers a hundred and fiftieth edition of Sweet Nell of Old Drury more attractive than Isaac Newton had better avoid my plays: they are not meant for such. And anyone who is more interested in Lady Castlemaine's hips than in Fox's foundation of the great cult of Friendship should keep away from the theatres and frequent worse places," warned Shaw. Nevertheless, as he pointed out, he brought three of Charles's mistresses, Nell Gwynn, Barbara Castlemaine and Louise de Kéroualll on the stage "to relieve the intellectual tension," and in fact their interpolations and clashes keep the play on a lively level of argument without cheapening it. The Nell Gwynn of Eileen Beldon was particularly warmly characterized and the French Louise (always suspected by the English as a spy) bewitchingly played by that mistress of Gallic charm in comedy, Yvonne Arnaud.

The last act was a kind of gentle *coda*, a scene played solely by Charles and his Queen, Catherine of Braganza, between whom Shaw imagined a quiet, understanding kind of relationship untouched by his intrigues, and in which he could reveal his tiredness, his disillusions and his plans without Court sham. Perhaps, in a sense, it was Shaw and Charlotte as their companionship had developed with the serenities of age: Shaw had touched on a similar relationship in *The Apple Cart*. It was well played by Ernest

Thesiger and Irene Vanbrugh, although Thesiger was by nature and temperament unsuited to the highly masculine part. Shaw was occasionally surprisingly blind in these things: his own approach being mental, it was on this level he judged his actors, and certainly Thesiger had long proved himself a reliable Shavian actor by these standards. A brief but brilliant performance was given by Alexander Knox in an entertaining character sketch of the sour-minded James, Duke of York (later James II). Trouncer was a superb Newton, giving the scientist's mentality a cutting edge and propounding his theories with characteristic wit and gusto.

Only one new play after the war held the London stage: a comedy, *Buoyant Billions*, with echoes of *The Millionairess* and *Back to Methuselah* (the rich girl "She" derives from Epifania, as the Chinese Priest from Confucius), not to count our old friend the Life Force. Written in 1946 and 1948, and first produced in London in 1949, its initial production had been, surprisingly, at Zürich in German. It is little more than a stew of earlier Shavian ingredients: yet it was not unlively in dialogue (remarkably so for an author well over eighty) and carried more wisdom still than one can find in any two plays by other dramatists of the time. In spite of slow, old-fashioned production it shone especially in the performance of Frances Day as "She." This magical blonde, a revue artist of few straight stage appearances, grasped the play's meaning with something more than a vibrant personality; for a few moments she and Shaw sent a sudden ray of poetry, like a silver moonbeam, spinning across the argument.

After his death she maintained in the press she was in spiritualistic communication with him. To the end Shaw's magnetism for women seems to have been capable of asserting itself; and who knows his questing, questioning spirit, having pierced beyond the veil, is not busily engaged in tearing it down?

Chapter 10

The Setting Sun

SHAW'S CREATIVE POWERS inevitably waned, as he was well aware: he went on writing because the established rhythm of his life could not after so many years be broken. A phenomenal worker, every day of his life, with a brain never still or at peace, writing was a necessity to him, as much as bread to another. He wrote fragments of plays until his death at ninety-four, and across these last thirty years of high fame poured out a steady stream of prose in the form of criticism, reviews, letters and pamphlets, many of course repeating earlier ideas (a great deal of his work is basically repetitive, though the style of expression never so). To the end he wrote with liveliness of mind and pen, most of his judgments proving more penetrating and prophetic as the years pass than was guessed at the time.

Two short books of his prime need mention: *The Intelligent Woman's Guide to Socialism and Capitalism* (1928), still a potent guide and encouragement to feminine political thinking, and the "fable," *The Adventures of the Black Girl in Her Search for God* (1932), which was attacked by the less enlightened clerical press but proved so popular as a serious attempt to clarify modern religious thinking that it sold over 200,000 copies within a year.

St. John Ervine says Shaw disliked traveling, and in a letter to Mrs. Pat in 1912 he wrote he was "the most deplorable of linguists" and "would rather write three plays than ask my way anywhere in a foreign country." Yet in the twenties and thirties his journeys across land and sea seemed incessant, including a world tour in 1932, sea cruises (one gave the idea for *Village Wooing* and the play was written on board ship), visits to America and the Soviet Union, and various appearances in Italy, France and other European countries. In Florida in 1936 he was filmed, and produced the expected Shavian sparkle for the occasion:

> It is no good in this country putting questions of national importance to me. I have been here before. I told you what to do, and you haven't done it. "Get rid of your Constitution." Have a good President and a bad Constitution and the bad Constitution gets the better of the good President all the time. The next thing will be that you will have a British Prime Minister.

The visit to Russia in the twenties, with Lady Astor, H. G. Wells and other political or sociological figures, was naturally the most controversial, and Shaw's refusal to propagate the myths desired by the West for purposes of anti-Russian propaganda met with distrust and abuse. But Shaw was not the kind to fake the evidence on either side; he was looking, as always, for the truth, and this in life makes for enemies on both sides of any curtain, iron or otherwise. He saw that Russia had achieved certain things impossible under the Czarist regime, and was shrewd enough politically to know—as with Hitler and Germany later—that when a people observes large benefits in the way of employment, building and industry it is not inclined too closely to look into the cost, either obvious or hidden below the façade.

This realist view, the only one really helpful to understanding the strength of an enemy and estimating the true forces needed to counterbalance his ideology, is too often resented, instead of being imitated, in the world of political thinking, and the warning applies equally to Soviet Russia and the United States today, in both of which wishful thinking about the weaknesses of the other side is at times so marked that it constitutes a real danger to peace.

Russian history had put that vast nation two centuries behind European and American civilization; the wrench needed to pull her forward into the contemporary world was the greater, and much bloodshed and human suffering, as well as much misunderstanding, inevitably ensued. Russia has never known democracy as we of the West understand it; the success of the revolution and its phenomenal powers of survival have depended on that.

Shaw always kept his historical perspectives clear, which is perhaps why he sometimes overlooked or undervalued factors outside them. Himself a man without cruelty or egoism in its wider sense of overriding and dominating other human beings, he was slow, as children are, to appreciate evil in others, especially when some of the results of their deeds seemed good. Nor did he (any more than Shakespeare) trust the multitude as a democratic force in itself, capable of thinking for itself instead of accepting what it was told by others. Universal suffrage was one thing, and no one fought harder for it than Shaw, and to practical purpose. But myths of this kind about universal wisdom and political aptitude seemed to him dangerous, supporting only acceptance of reiterated conventions. That is why at moments and to some it seemed as if he were supporting fascism or communism, though this was certainly not true in any political faction sense. Hitler he despised as an emotional neurotic, without till later realizing the full extent of the personal ruthlessness, and the immensity of the blind support the force of his personality could achieve. When he did realize it, it merely confirmed his suspicions of the unreliability of the political multitude.

Mussolini he rated as a better statesman, a verdict history now tends to support, for what that 'better' may be worth. Highly sensitive to cruelty or physical violence, his view of the Abyssinian War seems to have been bedeviled by his horror at some barbarities of mutilation (including castration) traditionally carried out by certain Abyssinian tribesmen on the bodies of their enemies. Never in his life did he support bombing in any form, but he was not the man hypocritically to idealize one side, and suppress knowledge of its barbarities, in order to blacken more deeply the other side.

The truths, as they became inescapable, troubled him deeply, as his letter to Mrs. Pat about *Geneva* shows. His only care, politically, was for the relief of human suffering and the raising of human dignity; and as far as man could progress from the animal to that end the better. Certain aspects of modern commercial life, with its pornographic insistence, through posters, advertisements and books, on sex as the ultimate goal in the freeing of the individual from outworn traditions, would have horrified and depressed him. His own crusades for feminine emancipation and a healthier, saner and less restrictive legal attitude towards marriage and divorce, in which the happiness of the parties was put before conventional shibboleths, were liberal and tolerant, but did not include an acceptance of promiscuity.

"I am fond of women (one in a 1,000 say)," he wrote to Ellen Terry: "but I am in earnest about quite other things. To most women one man and one lifetime make a world. I require whole populations and historical epochs to engage my interests seriously and make the writing machine (for that is what G.B.S. is) work at full speed and pressure: love is only diversion and recreation to me."

Small part though it played in his long life, however, he was no complete ascetic, and Mrs. Pat was not the only woman in later life to engage his (at least nominal) romantic interest. In 1921 a young American would-be actress and her sculptor husband, Molly and Laurence Tompkins, appeared on Shaw's doorstep at the flat in Adelphi Terrace, and Molly succeeded in getting herself invited in to tea, where she astonished and amused Shaw by propounding a scheme for opening a theatre in order to make his genius known to the world at large. This innocent American provincialism soon passed with the realization of how little, in Europe at least, Shaw needed this kindly propaganda on his behalf; but the friendship blossomed. Shaw saw her at dramatic school and in plays, criticized her performances, and kept up a prolonged and lively correspondence, with occasional meetings, until his death.

There is no doubt the young lady, who had a dark beauty not unreminiscent of Mrs. Pat's and a seductive temperament (Shaw proclaimed) to match, attracted him to some extent emotionally, for all his banter. That the friendship proved so lasting is also a tribute to the fact that she had a mind (later, she turned quite successfully to painting, and Shaw from her letters, which have not, unlike his own, been preserved, always maintained she had writing gifts). He was too old for romance, as he constantly (perhaps too constantly) pointed out to her; but on her side the affair seems to have had certain crises that reacted uneasily on him, without ever inducing him to cease the association. He warned her off wanting to accompany him to Russia (the suggestion seems to have been his, before he realized it was to be with a purely political group), and after her divorce evinced a certain amount of comical alarm.

Yet his letters acknowledge the charm. "I hoarded my bodily possessions so penuriously that even at seventy I had some left; but that remnant was stolen from me on the road to Baveno and on other roads to paradise through the same district," he wrote her in Italy. "I gather there are moments when your thoughts (or dreams) turn to me; and I am glad that there is still something immortal for you to turn to. It is hard for me to write letters now; but I can always read them when the Italian postmark is on them."

He and Charlotte had stayed in Stresa and visited the Tompkins on their island (Isolini) in Lake Maggiore.

There were picnics, long walks, counter-visits, and a state of polite tension between Molly and Charlotte that seems passably comparable with that between Mathilde Wesendonck and Wagner's wife Minna near Zürich. Shaw was amused rather than ruffled by this. Generally Charlotte, who loved travel, was the driving force behind their tours abroad, and it may be it was one of her ways of getting him away from other women (he had many admirers) and alone to herself. Jealous throughout her life, and suspicious of other women, the failure of her plans on these Italian occasions probably did not improve her manners or temper. Molly felt the strain, obviously returned dislike for dislike; and there are signs that Shaw, not now as violable as in the Mrs. Pat affair, put his foot down enough on Molly's behalf to preserve some kind of truce without spoiling his innocent flirtation.

When the Tompkins lost their money in the Wall Street crash, he paid for the continued education of her son Peter at Stowe School, the while upbraiding her not totally unseriously for "husband-stealing." "You are a coquette according to the classical definition: that is, a woman who deliberately excited passions she has no intention of gratifying." The echo again is of Mrs. Pat, and Shaw's weak spot for enchantresses of this order may well have solidified his content to remain married to Charlotte, an anchor who made no upsetting physical demands on the "writing machine." Flirt he could and did, not without trouncing his would-be seducer (as he had trounced Mrs. Pat), all as part of the not unenjoyable game.

The friendship never entirely blew cold; Molly after and even during her crises (in one she had attempted suicide) made no extravagant protests or demands, and he reserved for her an apparent affection less sorely tried than with Mrs. Pat. So candid, indeed, was the relationship that after his wife's death he told her, "We can write more freely now that Charlotte can never read our letters," although a year later he was writing with alarm: "I have just received your letter, with its proposal to come across the ocean to live with me. The same idea has occurred to other women. Put it out of your very inconsiderate head at once and forever, as they had had to."

He was, in fact, ninety years old. "I have had enough of marriage, and am quite happy alone, as I inherit from my mother a great capacity for solitude in my own company." But this was very soon after Charlotte's death, and the strain of isolation told more later. Her death in 1943 moved him far more than he had thought possible. A long illness from a bone disease had paralyzed her, so that moving her up and down stairs had become a burden on the household, and Shaw felt the physical relief from the strain after her death. "Her four years illness threatened to have a dreadful end; but a miracle intervened; she suddenly became younger than I had ever seen her, and incredibly beautiful, and had thirty hours of ecstatic happiness before she ceased to breathe," he wrote to Molly. To Barker, he added, "She was 86. I am 87."

They had lived in London at No. 10 Adelphi Terrace, Charlotte's flat, for many years, until in 1927 it was demolished with the rest of Adam's Adelphi under town planning orders, and they moved to No. 4 Whitehall Court, also with views of the river. Their main center was the country house, Shaw's Corner, at Ayot St. Lawrence in Hertfordshire, which they took early in the century and where Shaw remained until his death: writing day by day in a summerhouse in the garden, and taking interest from time to time in village life and his neighbors. After his death it became part of the National Trust.

He was active to the last, and indeed in the thirties and much later developed an even greater personal popularity in film interviews and newsreels, on television and on radio. He made his first broadcast on November 20, 1924, when he read his play *O'Flaherty, V.C.*; and thereafter his

Irish brogue and genial wit scintillated across the air and on screens of all sizes. Like that other great wit, Sir Thomas Beecham, in public his repartee was a source of enjoyment, both to himself and his hearers, and never carried a sting. And like his great contemporaries or near contemporaries, G. K. Chesterton, Max Beerbohm and Gordon Craig, he overshadowed other broadcasters in magnetism of personality and mind.

His friendships included people in all walks of life and some of the greatest figures of our time, in politics and the arts. Elgar was a close friend; Epstein and Rodin sculptured busts of him; John painted him. His generosity helped the famous maker of old musical instruments, Arnold Dolmetsch, to carry on his work at Haslemere in Surrey, with its festivals of early music; for he knew, none better, that specialist artistic work is never financially rewarding and quality and importance in the arts are not to be judged by commercial success. His generosities were great and never publicized. Flora Robson has told me of the unknown young actor in need to whom Shaw, when he heard of his difficulties, instantly gave one of the "prompt" copies of his plays, which with his own marginal notes he knew would fetch a good price if sold. He had the very rare generosity, St. John Ervine says from personal knowledge, that offers help before it is asked, and many benefited from this, for it was always tactfully given.

His thoughtfulness extended to all classes. Not long before his death, Sybil Thorndike told me, she drove down to see him with a Cockney driver who on hearing she was visiting Shaw showed great interest and excitement. Shaw, when she told him this, insisted in spite of cold weather in going out to the gate to speak to the man, and charmed him by asking many pertinent questions about the car and its running. (The creator of Henry Straker, dedicated chauffeur in *Man and Superman*, had been a car owner from the automobile's first invention.)

It has been said he lacked a feeling for natural beauty but this is not supported by what he wrote about Torca Cottage, seaside Irish home of his boyhood, or by passages in some of his letters.

". . . I drove into Dublin to-day and cursed every separate house as I passed. All the old longing for beauty and blessing gets stirred up in me . . ." he wrote to Mrs. Pat. "This house [Kilteragh, Co. Dublin] is just like a picture by Picasso; and it is right in the focus of the circle of hills from Killiney, where I dreamt my boyhood away on the East, to the Three Rock Mountain on the West. And oh! the shapes of those hills! . . . Oh! the two beauties I was born to love! Ireland's and Italy's, how they scorch my veins."

To Molly Tompkins he made even the view from Whitehall Court sing:

> This place is rather wonderful at night, with its posts in the skies and its panorama of the river from St. Paul's to Westminster. When the roads are black wet, and the embankment lights and car headlights are pouring floods of gold down them, there is really nothing like it in the world.
>
> I am alone tonight (Charlotte is in the country); and if you would just ring at the door—

She did not ring. But she preserved all his letters, and died in Atlanta in 1960, at the age of sixty-three, while helping her son Peter to prepare them for publication.[1] It is extraordinary that the friendship escaped attention so long; no biographer of Shaw had ever mentioned it.

Shaw died at Ayot St. Lawrence, where he had asked to be moved after a short period in Luton Hospital, following an accident in his garden when he slipped and broke a leg while pruning a tree. The date was November 2, 1950. He was ninety-four years of age.

[1] *Letters to a Young Actress*, edited by Peter Tompkins; *Shaw and Molly Tompkins*, edited by Peter Tompkins, Anthony Blond, London, 1961.

He died serenely, and without regret. "Well, it will be a new experience, anyway," he said to Eileen O'Casey, a visitor, an hour or two before he died. His work was done, and for some time he had made it clear to a few close friends that he was tired, and ready to go. "I have given up producing," he had written to Mrs. Pat in his last letter to her, eleven years before. "I am too old, too old, too old." And to Molly Tompkins, in 1948:

> My life now passes in a routine that never changes. . . .
> You must cast me off like a laddered stocking, and get a younger correspondent.
> Dont think, however, that I am forgetting you.

His last extant note to her was a verse on the back of a picture of himself at the gate of Shaw's Corner:

The Old Man at his gate
As he was in forty eight
And still is at ninety three
Awaiting news of thee
Molly Bawn.

Now the public mask of youthful resilience, preserved so long, too was shed.

He had refused all honors and titles (except the Nobel Prize for Literature in 1925) because they conflicted with his democratic principles; and he was not given a Westminster Abbey burial, perhaps because his will had asked for his ashes to be mingled with Charlotte's and scattered in the garden at Ayot St. Lawrence—though the wording, as St. John Ervine points out, had left an alternative open to his trustee. He had himself been instrumental in getting Irving buried in Westminster Abbey, and had tried to do the same for Lawrence of Arabia.

His death brought the usual panegyrics and the usual spate of detraction from lesser men and writers; none of which has made the slightest impact on his theatre reputation in practice. His plays are constantly revived throughout the world, and still enjoyed and supported by the public: he would agree with Wagner, who found the same discrepancy of attack by certain critics and popularity with audiences, that the public's is the only verdict of value in the long run. On Broadway, theatres observed a few minutes' silence on the news of his death.

The letters to Mrs. Patrick Campbell have been adapted for the stage in an entertainment, half public reading, half acted sketch, by the American-Irish actor-writer Jerome Kilty. Entitled *Dear Liar*, they were read and acted in London with considerable success by himself and his wife, Cavada Humphrey, as Bernard Shaw and Mrs. Pat, in New York by Katherine Cornell and Brian Aherne, in Paris by Maria Casarés and Pierre Brasseur, and in Germany by Elisabeth Bergner, who had been the first German Saint Joan.

The Shaw-Ellen Terry letters have been recorded by Dame Peggy Ashcroft and Cyril Cusack, and in that form sold all over the world. At Christmas, 1961, I saw the record prominently displayed in the window of a shop in the Kurfürsten Damm in West Berlin. "Nothing short of a masterpiece" was the verdict of the *New York Herald Tribune* on this recording.

In Ireland, always slow to appreciate home talent that flowers on alien shores, his plays have been kept alive in the theatre by Cyril Cusack in a steady stream of productions; and it was Cusack who provided the rose trees with theatrical names—Ophelia, Madame Butterfly, etc.—that now festoon the ascent to Torca Cottage, where the boy Shaw enjoyed such imperishable sunsets. Nevertheless, the Irish tend to preserve their sturdy independence of judgment about genius that has the effrontery to prefer to bloom in Britain, whether it be O'Casey's or Shaw's. "Ah, there's too much bloody *cynicalism* about that fellow!" a

Dublin docker was overheard to remark of Shaw in a pub. No one would have enjoyed the remark more than Shaw himself.

Today his reputation survives all denigration: his works not only conquer time but in many cases re-emerge as more prophetic, more apposite and alive, than they appeared to be when they were written. An actress, Dulcie Gray, playing Lady Utterwood in *Heartbreak House* in London eleven years after his death, has remarked in a television discussion that his parts for women are "extremely rewarding," not, as has sometimes been suggested, too obviously written by a man. "It is a *woman* talking. Shaw knew *all* about this kind of woman."

J. C. Trewin has referred in a fine phrase to his "mind of multiple candle-power." The French actor Jean Blanchard, in a tribute in Cusack's Shaw centenary program of *Androcles and the Lion* in Dublin in 1956, wrote:

> *Car chez lui, comme dans tout ce qui est irlandais, c'est l'humour qui toujours finit par triompher.*
>
> *Mais, au fond, l'humeur n'est-il pas la chose la plus sérieuse et la plus vraie du monde, dans ce monde qui se prend si volontiers au sérieux? Nous sommes redevables à Shaw de nous enseigner à ne pas nous prendre au sérieux, et lui non plus.*
>
> *Oui, assurément, il faut être intelligent, pour venir assister à une pièce de Shaw. Sinon on est roulé!*

"Some of the air we breathe now has G.B.S. in it, a little mountain oxygen that has somehow penetrated the fog." J. B. Priestley's is perhaps the tribute Shaw himself would most appreciate. For he wanted above all to clear that air, to make men think for themselves along new lines in a changing world.

His achievement was that he succeeded, and added to the gaiety of mankind while doing so.

Index